Living with Sight Loss

A Type 1 Diabetic's Life Story

by

Dianne Woodford

with

Jim McIntosh

Living with Sight Loss

A Type 1 Diabetic's Life Story

First published in 2016
by Dianne L. Woodford

ISBN 978-1-537249-15-5

In memory of my mum

Edna May Smith

CONTENTS

INTRODUCTION

What do you do when you wake up and your world has changed? Your first reaction might be to try and change it back again.

This was certainly my first thought on Sunday 26 August 2007 when I woke up to find that I had lost the majority of my sight.

I could make out where my window was and that it was light outside. However, for some reason I couldn't see items in my bedroom clearly and I felt like I was shrouded in darkness. My brain was certainly confused.

I tried rubbing my eyes but to no effect. I wondered whether maybe my eyes didn't want to wake up at the same time as my body this morning.

I got out of bed and stumbled and felt my way to the bathroom. I felt scared as I washed my face with cold water, rubbing water on my eyes in particular.

I then looked in the mirror but couldn't see myself. It was although the mirror was steamed up after a shower or bath. So I went through the whole process again. Still nothing. So I repeated it another two or three times.

And then I did what I would normally do when needing to think through a big issue affecting my life. I put the toilet seat down, sat down and tried to work out what I should do next. I started to accept that something may have drastically changed.

I wondered about how I should tell my parents and children? I certainly didn't want them to feel the stomach churning sort of panic that I was feeling.

I decided to go to my daughter Ella's room. Everything seemed to be happening in slow motion, as I was unable to do things at my usual pace.

I said 'hi' to Ella in my normal cheerful voice. After asking her the usual things such as had she slept well, I mentioned that when I had woken up I couldn't see very well. However, I pretended that nothing was seriously wrong to save her any unnecessary anguish.

I eventually phoned my friend Joanne and she helped me to drop all three children off at my parents'.

I tried to keep up the pretence that nothing was really wrong with my mum. She saw through this and told me I should go straight to hospital and get it seen to.

Funnily enough I didn't see it as an emergency as, apart from the sight problem, I felt well.

When we reached the Eye Hospital, which is part of Hull Royal Infirmary, I was taken for an assessment. I was taken into a room, was offered a chair and asked to read the letters on one of those standard sight test boards used by opticians. I was three or four feet from the board and realised that I couldn't see the board at all and I needed to ask where it was.

I was still expecting to be given some eye drops that would help my eye sight to return. However the doctor explained that I'd had big bleeds in the back of both eyes. Laser treatment and surgery were mentioned as options that might help my sight return but they couldn't guarantee that. An appointment was arranged with a consultant for the following week.

Joanne took me home. I was feeling tired and drained and just wanted to go to sleep as I had a horrendous headache brought on by trying to move around without sight all day.

The children and I had a takeaway for tea as I was not up to cooking.

As I went to sleep that night I was trying to stay positive about it and hoped that when I woke up the next morning it would have started to get better already.

This was my way of coping but as I'll explain later, my life had changed forever and I was going to have to come to find a way of still being a single mum to three children in a new, unfamiliar world.

BECOMING DIABETIC AT THE AGE OF 13

My story starts around the time of my 13th birthday. I was the fourth of my parents' five children, and they had also somehow found time to adopt another child. Her name was Michelle and I have always referred to her as my sister.

We were a normal working class family living in Hull. We were brought up to respect our elders, and anybody from a different race or with a disability. I also remember that we had to be very ill for my mother to allow us time off school.

All the girls shared a bedroom - my three older sisters Yvonne, Doreen and Wendy, Michelle plus myself. Our brother, Paul, was the youngest and was unfortunate in the respect that he had five girls to live with, but at least he had his own room.

We were a close family although like all children there were fallings out as we grew up. So my life was much the same as any other 13-year-old growing up in Yorkshire.

Around this period, I started to feel very thirsty a lot of the time. I would drink at every opportunity which meant that when I was at school I often needed to rush out at the end of lessons as I would be bursting to go to the toilet. When I did need to ask to go during a lesson the teacher would shout, "next time go between lessons"! I was a quiet girl and this stopped me asking unless I was desperate for the toilet.

The sad thing was that after using the toilet I was then drinking as much water as I could manage from the tap to quench my never-ending thirst. The thought never occurred to me that this was not normal.

This also happened through the night. The bathroom was downstairs and so I would sneak out of my room, trying not to wake my sisters. Before I came back up, I would detour via the kitchen to drink pints of juice. During the day, I often heard my mum complain, "who has been drinking all this juice, it's meant to last a week".

This went on for weeks and although I felt terrible, I never thought to complain that I felt ill.

I was also losing weight so quickly that my clothes were dropping off me. This didn't affect me too much as I wasn't weight conscious as a teenager. As a family we didn't even own a set of bathroom scales. I found out later my mother was asked if I had anorexia.

The first time that my mum took me to the doctor's in connection with these issues was one morning after I hadn't made it to the bathroom in time and my uniform was wet. Very embarrassing for a 13-year-old girl and I didn't want my siblings or anybody to know. Even after 33 years, this was a moment that I always remember.

Mum had an inkling that I was the 'juice thief' and she was aware that I was losing weight. But I think she put this down to teenagers and their hormones.

I had to explain what had happened to my uniform to Mum. As I only had one uniform, I couldn't go to school. So Mum said "enough is enough, we're taking you to see the doctor".

This was a rare occasion to be firstly out of school and secondly to be taken to the doctor's. There wasn't an appointment system, you just turned up and waited to see the doctor.

He was an old male doctor and it turned out that he was diabetic.

The doctor said to Mum that he was concerned and I needed to go back to the evening surgery with a urine sample. By this point Mum had miraculously managed to wash and dry my skirt and I went back to school in the afternoon!

I returned to the evening surgery and the doctor told us he would also need a blood sample. I was terrified of the blood test as I didn't like needles. Little did I know that this was going to become a daily routine. After testing the blood sample and putting a dipstick into the urine, he confirmed that I had become diabetic.

I didn't really know what being diabetic meant. I had recently seen a TV programme about cancer and someone losing weight. They had injections to help with their medicinal needs and in the back of my mind I thought that I had the same thing. It was a difficult time seeing my parents so upset.

The doctor couldn't get me into hospital until the next day. Mum was told to only give me minimal food and no drinks with sugar in until I was checked into hospital. I just wanted to visit my friends that evening and carry on as normal. I just really wanted to brush the problems away.

I went into hospital the next morning and stayed for several days whilst I received insulin injections and had a drip put in me. After a few days, they decided to teach me how to administer the insulin myself. The needles were different then; they didn't have the plastic disposable needles available today. Well they did, but the strange thing was that a diabetic child had to use syringes with steel needles even though the NHS had started giving plastic disposable needles, which were a lot smaller and nicer, out free to drug users. This was something that my mum had strong feelings about.

The thing that really upset me was missing the school play. I desperately wanted to get back to school as I had a good part in the play, which was Dick Whittington. The school said it was not a problem and they would find someone else to play the part but at the time that was really important to me. I had been chosen as I played the trumpet and my role would have been to announce people as they came on stage and playing a fanfare for the other actors coming on stage.

The hardest thing I think for my parents at the time was allowing me to go out with friends. This was before mobile phones as well. Would I remember to eat? What would happen if my blood sugars went low and I had a hypoglycaemic attack, which is where blood sugars become dangerously low and you could become unconscious if you didn't eat food containing high levels of sugar quickly.

I was a typical teenager and could be forgetful, get busy being with my friends and forget both the time and the need to take my glucose tablets, which could then lead to problems. I was trying to be normal and as I didn't want diabetes, trying to ignore it was my way of managing it.

When you are running around a field and the world starts to spin, you become hot and your breathing changes then you realise that a lack of sugar is the issue. If I didn't have sugar or glucose, I found it difficult to ask friends for their sweets.

During this time my siblings and friends was also learning how to manage their new sibling/ friend.

For the first time I felt different from them all. My siblings stopped arguing with me for a while and my friends were extra nice but all I wanted to be was normal. I didn't want this. I went back to school and normal life. If it was ever going to be normal again.

Looking back on this time, I realise that it must have been hard on family and friends. To step back and watch me trying to be normal, yet failing. It was important to me to feel the same as I didn't want to be special. I didn't want to be the only child allowed to eat in class but most of all I wanted to go back to being the same old me.

It wasn't about the injections - I got used to those. It was the fact I stood out in the crowd. This led to feelings of depression and mental health problems.

To this day I find it hard to tell people that I am diabetic. It has gotten worse over recent years with all the media coverage about overweight people and Type 2 diabetes. People get the wrong message and assume that I must have been very fat as a child to get diabetes so young. In fact, I have Type 1 diabetes which is less common than Type 2, often appears during childhood and is not connected to obesity.

MENTAL HEALTH ISSUES

Mental health was, and to some extent still is, a taboo subject. My issues were more than just diabetes. They began to extend to my mental health and how to manage this very deep hole that I found I was living in. It was like a thief in the night and was eating away at my soul. Yet people just didn't talk about it.

I would wake up feeling fine but within minutes of opening my eyes it would all come flooding back. I now had diabetes, life had changed and it wasn't going to change back. I had a deep down feeling of anxiety. The anxiety was at such a level that I couldn't manage or hold it in.

Sometimes it felt like a sickness deep inside that was destroying me. And it was moving so fast that I couldn't control it even if I tried. It's such a bad feeling and very hard to describe. As it was difficult to describe and felt so big, I couldn't tell anybody how I was feeling. Life was never going to be the same again.

However, I don't want this chapter to read like I was just feeling sorry for myself. I understand there are so many people in a much worse situation than mine, but I just couldn't cope with the way I was feeling. Here I was. Dianne the diabetic. Aged 13-years-old.

The diabetes ruled and controlled me. I could be sat in the classroom at school feeling dizzy because I needed sugar but not wanting to eat as I didn't want to be different to other children. 'Let's forget it is happening' was my motto. I failed to realise that this was just going to lead me into more trouble and make me stand out even more.

So I put my head in the sand and tried to forget it ever existed. Anyone with diabetes will understand that you can't pretend you don't have it. Later in my life I learned to treat it with respect and that by looking after insulin and food, I could then get on with my life without thinking about it.

At the age of 13, I was angry about my situation and didn't know how to vent this anger. I was also grieving for my past life. I just wanted the diabetes gone forever. And whilst all these thoughts were swirling around inside my head, I still tried to put on a happy front. The sad thing was nobody knew I was hurting so much inside. It was like a hole getting bigger every day. The bigger it got the more I didn't want to share it, thinking that if I admitted it, it would only hurt more. I didn't really understand myself anymore.

I didn't want my family to see my pain as I didn't want them to see what was happening inside me and hurt them.

I found that the hardest part of adjusting to life as a diabetic was not the diet or insulin injections, but the mental challenge knowing that I was now different to other children.

Before the onset of diabetes, if I had been asked what the hardest part would be then I would have said the injections, as quite simply I was terrified of needles. However, I soon got used to injecting myself with insulin.

But the mental side of being different to other children was the main issue for me. It wrapped itself around me like a fog. Whatever I did, it took over my life. And it followed me everywhere I went.

It was like it was my own personal fog. I never seemed to be able to get away from thinking about it. Even in my dreams, or perhaps they were really nightmares, I just could not get away from it. It took over my life and led to some very dark days.

Although I regularly attended a diabetic clinic, I didn't receive any counselling for the mental side of things. Looking back, it would certainly have helped me.

People didn't realise that I felt broken inside because I kept the fact that I was hurting badly away from everybody. I just kept it to myself and I'm sure that nobody knew. In fact, I went out of my way to show a happy front.

To this day I'm not sure why I never let people know at the time. Thinking back, I know that I didn't want to upset anybody and I didn't want to be a failure.

School became a real struggle. Other children said it wasn't fair that I could eat in the classroom and they couldn't and that was a really big issue for me at the time. I was struggling on a daily basis, living in my own self-made fog. I remember a teacher asking me if I was being bullied. But that wasn't the case. I didn't have friends but that was because I never made the effort to make friends.

Many aspects of teenage life, such as making friends just seemed like too much hard work whilst I was living with this fog constantly around me. Deep down I just didn't want to do anything. I lost respect for myself and I didn't care what I looked like. My hair went unwashed and I didn't worry about the clothes I was wearing. I had little interest in food. I just didn't want to eat normal meals, but that didn't help my diabetes.

The only food I seemed to want was sweet cakes from the local bakery so I would sneak out and go and buy doughnuts or cream buns. Sweet treats like this didn't help me control the diabetes and it was like I had a self-destruct button.

Mum and Dad's ruling was that we all had to go school unless we were very ill. I was ill inside but I didn't understand this. In fact I didn't see myself as ill at all.

Going out anywhere was a big trial at that stage and I would much rather have stayed at home in my own secure nest. I liked to sit in my room, listen to music, and pretend that I was anybody but myself.

At this stage I was also becoming very paranoid. If I saw the news and nuclear weapons were mentioned, I would think that a nuclear war was going to kill my family and I would be left to die a slow and painful death. This was the time in 1981/2 when the Greenham Common Women's Peace Camp and the protest against the government's decision to base cruise missiles there was on the news all of the time.

The school was concerned about me because I was very down at the time but nobody could get me to admit this. I just kept it all deep inside but eventually I was referred to the mental health team.

This was embarrassing for me because I felt a fool. Did they think I was going mad? I didn't want to have to deal with both diabetes and the fact that the doctors thought I was going crazy. I worried even more about upsetting my parents. I was making matters worse.

When I saw the mental health doctors they thought it would be a good idea to put me on Valium. The tablets just made my head feel really crazy which made life even more difficult. It is now known that Valium has a strong addictive affect but this was something my parents and myself weren't made aware of.

Mum used to bring the Valium tablets up in the morning to take with a drink. She was desperate to see me improve and when I look back now it must have been hard on her. She was trying to help me feel better but that wasn't easy as I didn't understand myself anymore.

Around this time, I do remember that at the Christian youth group that I attended, we had a lady speaker who told us that in times of difficulty we shouldn't rely on anything other than God to make us feel better. She then talked to the group about not needing medication or turning to drinking to solve our problems. That hurt me as I was relying on Valium, which is a strong drug especially for a 13 and-a-half-year old girl.

I wanted to ask, 'Why wasn't God making me better? Was I failing as a Christian? Had God turned his back on me'?

I decided to stop taking the Valium tablets and used to hide them under my pillow. I was in big trouble when Mum eventually found them all. Again I must have been wanting her to find them as I could have flushed them down the toilet. Maybe this was my cry for help? It was also another example of not telling people how I felt. Rather than just saying I don't want to take them, I didn't address the issue head on and just put the tablets out of sight.

Looking back, I am glad that I later decided to stop taking the Valium, given what I know about the history of the drug.

If you are reading this and are on medication for mental health issues or depression, then please don't follow my example and stop taking the medication. The drugs in use today are so much better than thirty years ago and the issues that I had at the age of 13 should not occur today.

I turned 14 in September 1982. The issues kept building up and in my head all I wanted was to turn the clock back one year and get rid of the diabetes. It all seemed so big and overwhelming that I would have this condition for rest of my life.

I was only 14 but already I could not see myself in my 40s. I couldn't see what I would be like the next day, never mind in years to come. I didn't respect myself in the present time and so I certainly wasn't thinking about, and probably didn't care about, what I would be like in the future.

It felt like I forever had my own personal fog surrounding me, that I would never be able to shake off. How was I going to keep up with this dark world? How long could I pretend I was happy?

At the diabetic clinic, the specialist nurses kept reminding me that if I didn't stick to the diet and do things right then eventually I might have complications and lose my sight, have a heart attack or my kidneys might fail. Or I could lose my feet or toes. I felt this condition was eating away inside of me.

Knowing that all these things could happen as I got older was overwhelming for a 14-year-old. I found that going to bed and being able to sleep and forgetting about it was a good option at the time.

However, sometimes I would lie awake at night thinking about nuclear war as my brain refused to switch off. It was like my brain was full of knots and nothing seemed straightforward anymore.

I felt like I was a real burden to my parents at this time. They were doing their best to help me and I was just hurting them by not getting better and not learning to live with the diabetes. I couldn't see an end to my problems. I was at a real low ebb and one day I decided to take a load of insulin and I would drift off and float up to heaven and everything would be ok. It would be like a big lovely sleep and sleep was what I wanted to do all the time to get away from the diabetes. I wasn't scared about doing this. In fact, it seemed the best answer to my ever-growing problems. I thought my family would be better off. My brain was very foggy and I couldn't see any other way out.

So I calculated how much extra insulin I would require to make myself really ill to the point of death and I overdosed on insulin. Whilst it probably made my parents' lives an awful lot worse, at the time I felt as though I was doing something good for them. I took the overdose one morning before I went to school using a mixture of long-acting and fast-acting insulin. I knew that it would probably be about lunchtime until it started to have the full effect. I looked forward to the relief of not having to live my life anymore.

I cannot remember all the details but I became very ill and was rushed to hospital by ambulance. I do recall that I was very cross when I came round as things hadn't worked out as I wanted. In fact I had only made things ten times worse. I hadn't found the relief I was hoping for and I was angry that I had failed in life again. I couldn't even end my life without making a mistake.

The hospital put me on a glucose drip to negate the effects of the overdose and in order to stabilise me. I remember the nursing staff being very cross with me and they told me I had wasted the time of the NHS.

Once I was better, I went home. My parents really didn't know what to do now and supervised my insulin injections. I just became more down and the fog just got thicker.

After a series of appointments with the mental health team during the next few weeks, I became an in-patient on the psychiatric ward at De La Pole Hospital for four months.

I have never really talked before about these months of my life because, as you will appreciate, talking about mental health issues is normally taboo. By writing these pages, I want people to know that it's ok to have problems with mental health. I have moved on and I can even say it made me a better person.

At De La Pole, we did activities such as baking and cooking and we talked with the staff whilst we did the activities. This helped me explain my feelings and concerns and didn't feel like counselling. Talking became easier over time and as it came out, the fog in my head started to clear.

The time away from school and general life helped and it also made me realise that I wasn't the only one with problems. Looking back, it was a huge step towards me accepting that I was diabetic. I grew to understand and learn the importance of taking control of it rather than the diabetes controlling me.

It was also around this time that I stopped thinking about diabetes all day, every day. I discovered that I just needed to think about it enough to keep it controlled. I found it hard when the time came to leave De La Pole as it had become my safe-haven. By the time I left, I was strong enough to move on with life. There was a bit of me that worried it would all get bad again and I would go backwards. But this didn't happen.

Rather than return to my existing school, it was decided that I should go to a smaller school – Kingston school - which sadly is now no longer there.

I made new friends and began to manage my life. I started to take control of the diabetes and it was no longer the first thing I thought of in the morning. Now I respected it and looked after it but it was no longer the be all and end all of my life. I could do different things. It wasn't all plain sailing but I had learnt so much about me and how I felt, that I managed to enjoy what life had to offer.

At Kingston school I took five O levels and was really pleased to win an award from my Social History teacher. I also won an award for the materials I made as part of the Childcare O level. I gained the respect of the teachers, which meant a lot to me.

I left school after completing my O levels. I wanted to go into nursing but couldn't do that until I reached the age of 18. So instead in 1984 at the age of 16, I went to college to do a Social Care course. I felt that leaving school was the right thing for me to do and hoped that college would enable me to grow up and move on with a view to finding my first job.

This period that I have outlined over the last few pages was a difficult part of my life, especially as I was a teenager dealing with mental health issues, but it made me the person that I am today. It made me a very strong person and most importantly I learnt to embrace and enjoy life. You can move on and I hope that reading about my experiences helps anyone living with their own fog. As for me, I learnt how to enjoy my life to the full.

WORKING LIFE

Going to college turned out to be a great move for me and in fact led to getting my first job much earlier than I could ever have hoped.

More importantly, I left behind the girl who didn't want to be thought of as different because she had diabetes. I was in the adult world and people in the adult world expected me to manage my diabetes. This expectation on myself made me look at my diabetes from a responsible adult way. Finally I was in control of the diabetes. It had stopped controlling me.

I started at Beverley College in September 1984 doing a course in Social Care. Little did I know at that time that I would end up living in Beverley many years later.

As well as the usual lectures, the course also involved practical work experience assignments. To be honest, I hoped to get one of the assignments that involved working in a children's nursery but instead I was selected to do work experience at an old people's home. I was not prepared for how physically demanding this job was going to be but was very proud of myself for being able to manage the insulin and my diet during very busy and energy-sapping days.

I was 16 going on 17 and used to travel to the home, Westfield House at Willerby, near Hull, on my bicycle. What I soon discovered was I had found my niche and really enjoyed the work.

I also really liked the people that I worked with. The other staff were all older than me but each one took me under their wing and I enjoyed being treated like an adult and no one saw an issue with my diabetes. In fact the staff munched their way through far more biscuits than I did and never worried about it.

I quickly found that I had the necessary patience and was really good at looking after old people. This gave my confidence a real boost.

The assignment was supposed to last six weeks but when the time came to return to college, I was offered a job and took it. The only downside was that I never actually completed the college course.

I ended up working as a Care Assistant at Westfield House for three years and enjoyed every minute of it. I was contented, found out who I was and was getting a wage packet doing something that I loved.

However my ultimate ambition was still to be a nurse and working as a care assistant only strengthened my desire to pursue a nursing career. I knew what the role was about as one of my sisters was a nurse.

I eventually applied for a nursing job when I was 19 and after several interviews, was offered a role.

I was surprised to find that being a diabetic didn't affect me gaining a nursing job. In fact it gave me more understanding of how it feels being a patient. To this day, I believe if you have had to spend any time as a patient in hospital it helps you to be a better nurse. Being a patient in hospital can make you feel very vulnerable. One of my core values when I was nursing was that I always treated patients as I would treat my own mother, with great respect.

Finally, my first day on ward as a nurse arrived and when someone shouted 'nurse', it was me who they wanted assistance from which felt very scary. At least I was on familiar territory as the ward I was assigned to was for elderly people.

I soon got used to hospital life. The nurses all helped each other and I quickly learnt the ropes and also witnessed some of the tricks played by the experienced nurses.

On one occasion, a senior nurse sent a new girl to ask for a long stand. She went downstairs to request this and was told to stand in the corner and was left some time. She got her long stand. I was just glad it wasn't me being tricked.

On one of my early days on the elderly ward I was involved in helping a patient get legless, in a funny sort of way. What happened was that a very jolly man asked for help with putting his socks on. As I pushed the sock on his leg fell off into my hands. As you have no doubt guessed, it was a false leg. As a nervous young girl it was a shock but the man saw the funny side and I did enjoy the patients with a sense of humour.

I always thought that dealing with death was going to be difficult and at times I worried about this in the early days. I became more accustomed to it as time went on.

I also got to understand about preparing a body after death in a respectful way and the duty of washing the body from head to foot which is the last task before the body leaves the ward. It was a very important role and I was very honoured to have helped with this many times.

Early on in my career, I always wanted to be working on the ward giving hands on care and wasn't interested in roles that would mean me being in an office doing paperwork.

To help keep the patients' spirits up, we had a record player on the first elderly ward that I worked on. I enjoyed singing the old time songs such as 'Roll Out The Barrel' and we often sang along as we worked. The dementia patients often surprised me as whilst they might not remember anything recent, they knew the words to many of the songs. Each year at Christmas, the staff would put on a Christmas concert and show for the patients. I would play the clarinet at such concerts.

Whilst I loved the work, the shifts were long and I also had the challenge of working night shifts and managing diabetes, which I did with assistance from the diabetic team. This involved swapping times for insulin injections and food to ensure my body could cope with the demands of the night shift. It was a challenge but I am proud to say I coped.

As well as working on the elderly ward, I did work on the burns unit for a period. I didn't enjoy this as much as I was squeamish and some of the sights you see there aren't nice. I also missed working with the elderly.

After eight years, I then successfully applied for a nursing role in the oncology ward at the Princess Royal Hospital in Hull in the mid-1990s. I really enjoyed my two-and-a-half years there looking after patients with cancer. The hospital was a small unit which was subsequently demolished.

Initially I was a bit nervous about how I would cope nursing young people who may be dying. However the work appealed to my compassionate side and I found that I was respectful of my patients' needs and wants and that it was an honour to be caring for them during their last weeks and days.

There was lots of laughter on the ward as well as tears and it was never a dull place to work. One day we even had a wedding on the ward, uniting a couple who wanted to be married. The lady died two days later but her wish of having a wedding came true.

At times when a patient that you were close to had died, I just wanted to cry when I got home. I also found that you got very involved with the patients' families and tried to be supportive and provide all the information they needed.

Though it was difficult, it was a privilege to help people during difficult times in their lives.

I worked what was known as the twilight shifts – early evening to 0300 and 0500 to lunchtime. It has to be said that these messed up my body clock and at times made it difficult to manage my diabetes.

I worked at all the hospitals in the Hull area whilst undertaking the above roles but my favourite was Kingston General on Beverley Road in Hull, a small hospital that subsequently closed down in 2001. Because of its small size, all the staff knew each other and it was a very close-knit community. I have great memories of working there.

I then decided that I needed a role away from hospitals where the hours were more suitable for a working mum with a young family such as myself. So I applied for and got a role as a District Nurse in

1996. This meant I was now a senior nurse visiting house-bound patients to provide advice and care and I was able to prescribe medication.

Because of the work involved, I found that the skills I had learnt during my time in the oncology unit were very useful in helping people who had decided they wanted to die at home. As you are visiting on a regular basis, you become part of the family and I enjoyed that.

One area that I found quite challenging was looking after some of the older patients who were diabetic, like myself. A number had lost toes or even legs which had needed to be amputated and so I saw first-hand where diabetes can go in later years. It was a definite wake-up call and I realised this could be my future and obviously it worried me having the same condition. Because I was still quite young, it seemed like a long way off and I hoped that I would be one of the lucky ones and it wouldn't happen to me.

In 2002 I moved to a role as a Practice Nurse at a GP's surgery as the hours fitted in better with school drop offs and pickups. One part of the role that I enjoyed was seeing the same patients week after week and building a rapport.

However there were new challenges for me to face. In particular the practice was in a poor part of Hull, north of the City Centre and a lot of the patients were either refugees or immigrants who spoke little or no English. Where this occurred, we had access to language interpreters via the telephone and some days I could be contacting the interpreter numerous times.

There was more administration to do as a practice nurse and indeed it was the first time that I was required to use computers as part of my day to day job as these were now used for writing up patients' notes.

I have always enjoyed the nursing role. It could be a challenge when combining it with bringing up two young children and running a house. However I always imagined that I would be a nurse for the rest of my working career.

It also meant a lot to me that my parents were both really proud that I battled against diabetes and sorted out my mental health issues and settled into a career. I did a lot of growing up during my working life.

Looking back on my time working in nursing, and in the oncology unit in particular, I met people dying at a very young age who never got to see their families growing up. So when I lost my sight a few years later and people said, 'it's sad you will never see your children grow up', I realised I was still lucky enough to be alive as my children were growing up.

THE FOG LIFTS

The fog that I talked about in my earlier years eventually lifted and has rarely returned and I am proud to say that I moved on. Overcoming the depression has also helped me deal with subsequent issues in my life.

Mental health is a difficult illness that can last for years. I am always aware that depression is very life-crippling and can take over both your own and your family's life. It can be a very dark tunnel and sometimes the light at the end of the tunnel can seem a long way away.

Over the years, I have met people with mental health problems and found them to be very nice and sensitive people. They are genuinely decent human beings who are fighting an illness that cannot be seen and I respect them very highly. Depression is often not seen as the crippling illness it really is.

Looking back, the reasons why I was able to manage my mental health was due to starting work, growing up, and my life generally moving in a better direction. I was a busy young woman and had no time to think about being depressed. I was also too busy enjoying my life.

After the awful period when I wanted to end it all, it didn't actually take too long for me to become more social. I learnt how to enjoy my family and friends.

This is not to say I still haven't had the symptoms of depression at times, and I know myself if I am starting to get down. When this happens, I have an action plan that kicks into place. For example, if being stuck in the house is getting me down, I go out for a walk or go and see a friend or family member. It's really that simple.

I also know that I can visit my GP at any time and have a discussion if it gets too bad. My message is: don't sit there on your own and dwell on it and let it build up.

What has become apparent to me is that the best way to manage mental health issues is to share your concerns with others in the same situation. This really helps. I do wish that Facebook had been around when I was a teenager as I would have used it to find out how others managed. It would also have helped me find out that I wasn't the only one with these issues. That would have been a great help.

I can fully understand the pressure placed on parents in these situations and I hope that I have been able to adequately share what I feel were the learning points from my own situation. No parent wants their child to go through mental health problems.

To people reading this who are either a parent with a diabetic child or who have a child with mental health issues, what I would say is that there is light at the end of tunnel and I grew up to be a normal working woman enjoying her life. So please take my word for it. These sorts of issues can, and do, come to an end.

MISCARRIAGES AND CHILDREN

My first marriage was to Graham and took place in October 1990. The wedding took place at Trafalgar Street Church on Beverley Road in Hull. I was 22 years old.

My mum had made me a beautiful wedding dress and we had a lovely day. With eight bridesmaids and two page boys, it was quite hectic with so many young and excited children around.

My parents did the catering and a friend of Graham's took the photos and it all came together well. We even had a couple of patients off the ward who were brought by some of my fellow nurses.

I left my parents' home for the first time and we moved into our first house. I found this quite difficult at first as I moved from a busy chaotic house full of people to a quiet house with just the two of us. My parents always had an open house and people popped in for a cuppa regularly. As I was part of a large family and with the arrival of numerous grandsons and granddaughters for my parents there was never a quiet moment, but I loved it that way. Having my new but quiet house was therefore very strange. But I also had the thrill of building my very own nest.

We had bought an old Victorian house in Albert Avenue, Hull about three months prior to the wedding and spent every spare minute doing it up and renovating it, ready for us to move in.

During our DIY efforts, there was an accident about six weeks before getting married that ended up with me in the casualty department at hospital with concussion. The accident occurred when Graham was up a ladder cleaning out some old lead-lined guttering, which can't have been well secured. I came out to ask if Graham wanted a drink and at this point the guttering came loose, fell and hit me on the head. It was six weeks before we got married so the joke between us was that he had already started trying to get rid of me.

And then, two weeks before the wedding there was another accident which required another hospital visit for me. I was unpacking the car boot and unfortunately Graham hadn't noticed me and shut the tailgate which caught my head. The best man did mention this in his wedding speech, suggesting I would need a crash helmet if I was to survive the marriage.

At this time, I was still nursing, working long shifts, which could be quite tiring. I cycled to work to save money on petrol and also took on a second job doing cleaning for someone to fund changes to the house. I certainly had no need to go to the gym as the two jobs combined gave me all the exercise that I needed.

My diabetes seemed generally to be OK, or so I thought. I was so busy it just seemed to be running in the background. The mistake I was making was letting my blood sugars run slightly high to stop me having hypoglycaemia attacks. The longer term effects of doing this would eventually cause future problems for me.

Our original plan was for both of us to work for a few years and save up to start a family. However, this plan didn't work out, partly due to my diabetes.

At that time, as a diabetic I was unable to get the full contraception pill. The policy was to put you on a mini pill. Well it didn't work, I got pregnant whilst on honeymoon.

Unfortunately, this ended in a miscarriage three months into the pregnancy in early 1991.

At a subsequent check-up six weeks after the miscarriage, I was over the moon to find out that I was pregnant again. I really had no idea that I was until they told me at the check-up.

At the time, Graham's family ran a garden centre and the consultant who was overseeing my care was a regular customer. So the joke used to be that we must sell very good fertiliser at the garden centre!

My excitement was mixed in with lots of worrying. As a diabetic, I faced additional challenges whilst pregnant as a mother's blood sugar levels are being shared with the unborn baby and so I found that I needed to be extra careful about what I was eating whilst pregnant. Diabetics are renown for having big babies that are not always very healthy.

I was forever testing my blood sugar levels to make sure they were at the right level and as a consequence, my fingers were always very sore. But protecting my unborn child was very important to me and my diabetes was always on my mind. At times it felt like it was taking over my life.

I was very scared of having a further miscarriage. Even though the first miscarriage was just one of those things and was not due to my diabetes, I still blamed myself for it.

So life outside of work generally went on hold to ensure that I did nothing to jeopardise my baby's health. I did everything within my power to protect my unborn child.

Around twelve weeks into the pregnancy, I was rushed into hospital in an ambulance with horrendous bleeding. The doctor who saw me said that in his view I probably had suffered another miscarriage, and they would do a scan the following day to verify his diagnosis. This news was devastating.

I spent a long night in hospital on my own worrying myself silly and thinking, "why me" and "why can't I have a baby". The night staff offered me strong painkillers to help with the cramping that had started to affect me but I refused as in my mind they would affect my baby. I couldn't accept that my baby had gone.

The morning eventually arrived and I was taken for the scan. As the monitor passed over my tummy, I looked up and saw a baby's regular heartbeat on the screen. It was the most amazing thing ever. Twenty-four hours earlier I had been told that it was unlikely that I was still pregnant and now I had the joy of knowing that my baby was fine. It is hard to express just how elated I felt and my tears of sadness turned into tears of joy.

Graham was late coming to the hospital and missed the scan but seeing my smiling face he knew it was good news. I was also glad that I hadn't taking the strong painkillers the night before. I was so protective of my unborn baby, eating the correct foods, not drinking alcohol and avoiding being around smokers.

I talked to my bump as it was growing and sang songs to it. I thought of the baby most of the time I was awake. I also enjoyed turning a bedroom into a nursery with paintings of Peter Rabbit and other Beatrix Potter characters that I did myself. Even though I worried about my unborn child, these were also exciting times and I couldn't wait to meet him/her.

The NHS kept a close watch on my pregnancy since I was diabetic and had had a previous miscarriage. I had regular scans and check-ups at hospital, on a weekly basis as the due date got nearer, and got a lot of support from the diabetic maternity team. The latter were really helpful and supported me dealing with all the issues that I came across as a diabetic mum-to-be. All the staff helping me were so lovely and made it all so much easier with their encouragement. As I went to the clinic with each pregnancy, I was going to the clinic for well over a year. It sometimes felt like one very long pregnancy.

An added complication was that during one of my check-ups, they established that the baby was in the breech position. The doctors spent time during that appointment manipulating the baby and they successfully got its head down and in position ready for labour.

However, by the time I got back home that evening it was evident that baby had other ideas and had turned round and gone back to being breech. This was one stubborn baby.

Ideally, I wanted a natural birth as I preferred the idea of doing it all yourself. The advice from the medical team was that due to a combination of the baby's breech position and the fact that I was diabetic, they wanted the baby to be delivered by Caesarean section. I was upset by this discussion but I would have done anything for the health of my baby.

I was booked in for a Caesarean at 0900 on 11 November 1991 and everything went like clockwork and by 0915 my first child, Eloise Amy, was born.

Given her date of birth, we did consider 'Poppy' as a name. However, I just always liked the name

"Eloise'. It just suited her and was a fairly unusual name at the time.

By pure coincidence it was also the title of a song released in 1985 by the group 'The Damned'. I only heard the song when Eloise was about six months old and I then went and bought the record. When she was young we used to dance together to this. Maybe I should say we rocked to it as parts of the song are fast and lively!

I also felt that the name would give Eloise different options on what to call herself in later life. As a teenager she chose to be known as Ella.

For the record, we never had a boy's name so maybe deep down my mother's instinct was that I was giving birth to a girl.

Anyway I am getting ahead of myself. Going back to the birth, this was by far the most amazing experience ever. Hearing my baby crying just after birth was like music to my ears. I did it. I was a mum. I couldn't believe it. I wish I could have bottled that feeling. It still brings me joy thinking about it. I still need to pinch myself today as to be able to give birth to a child and know that you have been involved in its creation as its mother is the most fantastic thing.

Ella was immediately taken away from me into special care as her blood-sugar levels were very low and causing concern.

Checking the baby's blood sugar level is done whenever mum is diabetic and is a completely normal process. As baby essentially will start with mum's blood sugar level there can be issues. In Ella's case they took her into special care to keep an eye on her. As this was the days before mobile phone cameras I did not even have a picture of my baby to look at. I just wanted her next to me and so those were the longest 24 hours of my life whilst I was separated from my baby.

I got to go into the special care baby unit the next day to see my baby for the first time. I thought she was the most beautiful baby ever and I had to pinch myself as I couldn't believe she was mine.

Fortunately, Ella's blood sugars returned to normal and we were re-united on the ward on day four. This was scary as she had had all the special care nurses caring for her and then it was just me. What if I made a mistake?

I tried my hardest to feed Ella myself and whilst it seemed to be working and it was certainly helping Ella and myself to bond, she was not gaining any weight. The midwife was very unsympathetic and basically told me that I wasn't doing a very good job. Nowadays I am sure that I would have received more support and encouragement.

Something that I regret was not asking anybody else once the midwife said breastfeeding wasn't working. I put her straight onto bottled milk. Looking back, I felt like I had given in without a fight. The experience certainly scarred me for a while. It would have helped to have a breastfeeding adviser on hand.

So I started feeding Ella by bottle as it made it easier to measure what she was having and ensure it was sufficient to put weight on. Despite these efforts, she still took a while to start putting weight on.

One obvious worry was if Ella would also have diabetes. As she grew up I was always concerned if I thought she was drinking too much. Like any mother, I was concerned about my child's well-being I suppose. I need not have worried as it turned out that neither Ella nor either of my two other children have diabetes.

The explanation for this is straightforward and I hope will stop other people worrying about it as well. My diabetes was juvenile diabetes and not hereditary in my case. My children now have the same chance as anyone else of being diagnosed with it later in life. My way of thinking though is if they had ever developed diabetes, it wouldn't be the end of the world. You can live a normal life with just a few adjustments.

My next two pregnancies ended again in miscarriages, and again it was never confirmed that these were related to my diabetes. Each time I conceived my blood sugar levels were within the normal range.

I became pregnant again in the summer of 1993. This turned out to be a very difficult pregnancy due to diabetes-related complications. My blood sugar levels would drop quite dramatically for no apparent reason quite regularly during the pregnancy. So I always had to ensure that I had a Mars bar and a bottle of Lucozade in my bag when I went out so I could have a quick sugar boost when required.

One day I had forgotten to put a Mars bar in my bag and I became so desperate for sugar whilst out shopping I must admit I rushed into a shop, picked up and ate most of the Mars bar before I had even got to the front of the queue to pay for it. This was a big move forward from the days when I would be embarrassed to eat a biscuit in a classroom.

It also didn't help that I had a toddler to look after so, as many mothers will be able to appreciate, I wasn't able to put my feet up and rest during the normal part of the day.

There was concern from the consultant and his team that the foetus was not growing as expected and that it was very small and weak. So they decided that I should use a Doppler heart monitor. This involved taking a trace of the foetus' heart rate once I was 22 weeks into the pregnancy and telephoning the test results through to the maternity unit on a daily basis.

As the due date got nearer, it became apparent that, due to concerns that the foetus may have stopped growing, I would be having another planned Caesarean around eight months into the pregnancy. This time I was more prepared for how it all worked.

Again the operation was due to be carried out at 0900. However, on that day, there were several other cases that were deemed more urgent and they jumped the queue.

Eventually I went into theatre at 1600. The seven-hour delay caused difficulty with my diabetes as I wasn't allowed to eat. Even though I was on a drip and the hospital did hourly blood tests, my diabetes was beginning to play up as my nerves were beginning to get the better of me.

To everyone's surprise the baby, a boy, weighed in at 9 pounds 10 ounces despite being four weeks early. This was the first of many surprises and jokes that my first son has played on me as he has grown into a character who enjoys surprising other people. To this day he always plays the joker card.

Again we didn't know the sex of the baby before the birth. We decided to call him Josiah although when he became a teenager he chose to shorten this to Jo.

Jo also went into special care after he was born. He screamed so much, he got his own room because he was upsetting the other tiny babies. Indeed, for those few weeks he would scream and cry for much of the time and the hospital staff were not sure why.

I started off breastfeeding him and found that night-time feeds are another challenge for a diabetic as you must remember to eat yourself during the night when feeding to replace the calories being given to the baby. This could be very tiring as Jo would take a long time to settle back down. The constant blood tests to check my blood sugar levels left me with very sore fingers.

After ten weeks of breast-feeding it was decided that I should try bottle feeding to see if this stopped Jo crying as it was thought that my diet could be affecting him and giving him colic. Settling my second baby was a challenge in itself. Eventually the hospital diagnosed that he was allergic to gluten and dairy products and this was why he was failing to thrive.

As a baby, Jo also had Febrile convulsions, where a child has a non-epileptic seizure or fit brought on my high body temperature, so we were in and out of hospital a lot. This made me very protective towards him as nobody likes to see their child hurting. I loved him so much that it broke my heart to see him in pain.

Being a working mum with two small children turned out to be very hard work indeed. Whilst Ella was more or less a model baby, Jo was hard work as it seemed like he was constantly crying. But I still loved them both equally. In a way, work was a relief as at least I got to sit down and have a cup of coffee at breaks in the peace and quiet.

I remember one fine summer's afternoon I had put Ella down for a nap in her bedroom but she started crying. I also had Jo in his silver cross coach-style pram in the garden and he started crying too. I knew that there was nothing wrong with either of them and they were only crying because they were tired and restless.

I was exhausted myself, so I made myself a cup of tea and sat down on the garden bench waiting for both children to settle. At this point, the old lady next door put her head over the fence and said, "did you know your babies are crying"?

I politely acknowledged her concern and explained that both children were very tired. This wasn't what I REALLY wanted to say to her, but we wouldn't be able to print that.

After Ella was born, one of my sisters helped with childcare which enabled me to go back to work. With two children I decided on a different arrangement and so after Jo was born, I started working the night shift at the hospital. This involved taking the children to school or nursery and then grabbing whatever sleep I could until they were due to be collected again.

My mum supported me wonderfully with this plan and had Jo on the nights that I worked. She had so much patience with Jo and she always seemed to understand him. She was my rock in Jo's early years.

Despite the diabetes, I had an amazing motherhood and adored my children. My advice to any diabetic mums-to-be is simply to work with your local diabetic team for a healthy outcome. Having diabetes is certainly not a reason or excuse to not have children.

Somehow we also found the time to do some foster care for Barnardo's. I suppose this was because I was enjoying motherhood so much. We fostered two children with severe physical difficulties on alternate weekends to give their parents a break. It was hard work but with lots of rewards. In particular it introduced my own children to understanding people with disabilities and how to deal with them and treat them with respect._I enjoyed this time and had so much joy from having these special children in my life.

So the end of 1999 approached. We were a fairly typical family of two working parents and two children (Ella, eight and Jo, six) that we adored. As the millennium approached, I don't think any of us could have guessed at what the next ten years would bring. If I could have looked into the future, the thought of sight loss would have scared me, so it's a blessing that I didn't know what was waiting for me around the corner.

BECOMING A SINGLE MUM

My relationship with Graham had been in trouble for some time. There was no single cause that led to the separation and neither of us were to blame. Our different working hours meant that we were spending less and less time together and gradually we just drifted apart.

Even when we were together, we would be doing separate things. It even got to the point where we watched TV in different rooms. So even when we were in the house together, which was not very often, we rarely found the time to talk. The resulting lack of communication was a big reason we drifted apart.

The strange thing was, we could both talk for England. I guess neither of us wanted to talk about the important things.

Having several miscarriages definitely put a strain on our relationship. I say this now because looking back, neither of us really shared our feelings. There was a lack of emotional support on both sides.

For my part I needed support but didn't think it right to lean on Graham and put him under more stress. He probably felt the same too.

The miscarriages caused such a deep hurt inside me that I didn't want to talk about the pain. It felt so raw and so I hated talking about it. I also blamed myself for not being able to carry a baby. I often thought it was my fault and this in itself made talking about it more difficult.

In fact, it took me many years to be able to talk about having miscarriages without getting upset.

Having diabetes that was hard to control was difficult for me to accept as I am a person who likes to feel in control all of the time. Having low blood sugars was always difficult as I had to stop what I was doing. This frustrated me then, and that remains the case today.

As I have said before I often let my blood sugar level run a little bit high to save me the bother with hypoglycaemia. This in itself was to cause me problems later on in life. At the time, this seemed a good idea but I have learnt the hard way. So to any young person with diabetes reading this and who is running high blood sugars, I hope you understand what I am saying.

I don't think that I met or spoke to older people who had a lifetime of experience with diabetes. A few words of wisdom from an experienced diabetic would have been invaluable to me at that time.

An early example of the sort of complication that I experienced was when I went for what should have been a straightforward tooth extraction. My wisdom tooth was removed on the Friday at the beginning of a Bank Holiday weekend. I got an infection, hardly unusual after an extraction. When I returned to see the dentist on Tuesday with a temperature and in a fair degree of pain, the dentist immediately called an ambulance and I was taken into hospital. What transpired was that as I was running high blood sugars, the infection quickly developed into septicaemia and I had become very ill and was kept in hospital for around a week.

Graham found this hard to grasp and when he got a telephone call saying his wife was in intensive care, I was told that his reaction was, 'who is going to cook my tea tonight'. I guess this was probably the first thing that came into his mind. But it was moments like this that I found very difficult to deal with.

I rarely felt 100 percent well due to the diabetes. It was very hard for Graham to understand the diabetes. I don't blame him for that as maybe I tried to deal with it myself and struggled to ask for help and say that diabetes was bothering me. I still wanted to be in control of the diabetes and didn't like to share the issues I was having being a diabetic.

Some of life's circumstances that I have mentioned above made things harder but I still believe we would have eventually separated even if I hadn't been diabetic and there were no miscarriages.

I had been thinking about separating for some time. However, it was not a decision you take lightly when you have two young children. But the tension between Graham and I was very strong and when I realised it was affecting the children, I made my decision.

There were no counselling services available to help us and so in June 2000 I moved out with the two children and went to live with a friend to clear my head and make decisions about my future. I was 31 years old.

The hardest thing ever was to tell the children that things were not going to be the same again. I worried about this to the point of illness. I just wanted my children to know how much they were loved. I knew in my own head that it was best for them in the long run but in the first few weeks it was difficult as the children wanted to know where their dad was and why both he and mum were upset.

Once I had made my decision, I knew I wasn't going to change my mind as I didn't think there was a way back.

Overall it was just a horrible time. I couldn't eat which, as a diabetic, was not a good place to be.

Fortunately, the children soon got into a pattern of going to see their dad on a regular basis and this carried on for a number of years until they were old enough to arrange when to see him themselves.

I did have some counselling myself, arranged with the assistance of my GP, to come to terms with the separation.

My first year as a single mum certainly had its difficulties. Although I was used to doing most of the childcare in any case, there were all the things I hadn't previously done and hadn't realised needed doing. So I had to learn how to change the car's water and oil and check the tyre pressures.

At times I did feel exhausted and on more than one occasion I took the children to the cinema to see a film and slept through it myself.

The hardest things were the events that you previously attended together such as parents' nights at school or when the kids were doing shows and things. I think we did quite well at either agreeing that we would attend these together or ensuring that we arranged separate appointments. Over the years we learnt to discuss things more, both moved on and eventually we both remarried.

Even though we were separated, both children saw Graham on a regular basis and still had a father figure in their lives, although at times I felt as though I was doing both jobs. I had a lot of support from my own parents which was really helpful. It was hard for the kids as they were splitting their time between several different houses, as I had moved again, although I'd like to think they also saw this as being a bit of an adventure.

I also like to think that as parents, Graham and I kept the issues with our relationship to ourselves once we had separated and that we were both quite relaxed with the children. I certainly didn't say anything bad about Graham in front of the children.

However, a very immediate impact for me was my circle of friends. Graham and I had many friends through a church group that we had been involved in. As they didn't agree with divorce and it was me who had instigated the split, I lost quite a lot of these friends.

My social life was mainly based around the children, in common with a lot of parents with children at this age. I made some new friends and met other mums with children of similar ages at the groups the kids went to.

I didn't have a lot of free time for myself as a single mum who was also working full time.

A general lack of my own friends made me a little bit vulnerable. I found that I was desperate to make friends and I probably made a few mistakes there as I was happy to make friends with anybody. I just needed somebody to love me.

A SECOND MARRIAGE AND
A THIRD CHILD

In April 2001, I met Andy, who was the brother of a friend I had made after my first marriage broke down. The relationship started off on the right footing. We got on well, laughed a lot and it all felt quite comfortable.

Andy had a daughter, Leanne from his first marriage who I loved from day one. She was so lovely and Ella and Jo really enjoyed her being around too. Indeed, Jo and Leanne even had their birthdays in the same week and they had a shared birthday party.

My mum treated her like any of her other grandchildren. Leanne became a big part of our family, and still is today.

For my 33rd birthday in September 2001, Andy took me to Paris as a surprise present. It was my first time in an aeroplane and was all really, really exciting.

I was worried about flying but soon learnt how to love travelling, experiencing a different culture and a foreign language.

I enjoyed seeing the different sites in Paris, which included a trip to Disneyland. I really enjoyed the magic of Disneyland. I even had a few photos of myself taken with some of the characters. I wished that I could have taken the children there as they would have been thrilled by it. I brought presents from Disneyland for them all but it still wasn't the same without them with me.

We then walked down by the river and had a drawing made of us both together. It was all very romantic and I felt I had found the man for me. To this day I love romantic gestures and poems.

And then, probably the most romantic thing that has ever happened to me, took place. We walked hand in hand under the Eiffel Tower and found a little bench. We sat down and Andy proposed to me on my birthday and I said 'yes'. I was giggling when he got down on one knee. I think the giggling was due to my nerves. I am not sure who was the most nervous. It turned out that Ella had helped to choose the engagement ring.

At this stage of life, I felt very happy and relaxed. We had a nice house and lovely neighbours.

We made all the arrangements and got married in May 2002. Looking back, it was all quite quick, really. At the time, I was head over heels in love and didn't really look beyond that. With hindsight, I probably should have done. You would think once bitten, twice shy.

But once I got involved in the arrangements, it all just happened and I ignored the reservations that I had deep down, assuming they were natural and I was just over-reacting.

Indeed, I was still hurting from my first marriage and thought I was nervous and concerned because of I had had a failed marriage.

I went into this marriage with the same approach as my first - that this would last forever. Indeed, I felt more mature so this time it was all going to be ok.

To be honest, there were no plans for us to have children. When Jo was born I had been told that I would need IVF if I wanted another baby. Our expectation was that we wouldn't have children and I wasn't trying for a baby.

I hadn't had a period for over two years so it was like nature was telling me that having another baby was not meant to be. I wasn't sad about this. I just accepted it I felt lucky that I already had two wonderful children and was now step-mum to an amazing girl. What more did I need?

Things were going along quite nicely for the first 18 months of the marriage. And then we both had a very big surprise in Spring 2004 when I found out that I was pregnant.

I had been putting weight on and my stomach was bloated. I thought that I had a cyst on an ovary, which was a problem that I had suffered from previously. So I went for an ultra-sound scan to see how big the cyst was and whether it required an operation.

It was at this point I discovered my own little miracle. The nurse doing the ultra-sound scan looked at the screen then turned to me and said, "there's baby's heartbeat." Even though the scanning device was sat on my tummy, I went into denial and said, "no, that's not mine," but she insisted, "this is your baby." And of course it was.

Whilst I was excited, I was also really nervous as my track record of pregnancies wasn't very good. Again, I had to be very careful with my blood sugar levels. I didn't want the children to find out too early and be excited about a new brother or sister in case it didn't work out. But they soon guessed by my ever growing tummy.

Andy was basically shocked by this unexpected development and he handled the news very badly. It was at this stage that the marriage started to fall apart. I don't blame the pregnancy for the break-up. It was something that was probably going to happen anyway at some point as the marriage was based on romance and after learning to live with each other for 18 months, the cracks had begun to show.

Ella, now 12, was very excited that her mum was having a baby. She was very maternal and straightaway wanted to help look after the baby when he or she was born. Jo wasn't so keen. I guess as a ten-year-old, the thought of a crying baby didn't appeal to him. I realised that this was a big adjustment for the children, as well as for myself. The house was small and Ella and Jo were used to their own rooms. I often wondered how it was all going to work out.

The pregnancy was exceptionally difficult as I got pre-natal depression. Even though I had nursing experience, I wasn't even aware that pre-natal depression could happen until I had it myself.

The fog had reappeared and I was beginning to feel out of control. Everything I was doing seemed so much like hard work. Even making a cup of tea left me feeling drained. And yet all the time I was trying to stay normal for the children, as the last thing they needed was me being unable to cope.

Ella once caught me crying and asked, "what's wrong"? My reply was that I just had a lot on my plate at the moment and she then said, "I understand it's hard when you are not hungry and still have to eat…" So although I was really excited about the fact that I was having a baby, the depression was still hard to handle.

At this stage, Andy was avoiding the situation and was often out for hours at a time, coming home drunk. I had great concerns about bringing a child into this situation.

The fun thing was choosing a name for the baby. I had found out at the 20-week scan that the baby was a boy so started to think about suitable names.

This was the first time that I had found out the sex of the baby before the birth. I didn't know the sex of either of my first two and it was left for a surprise when they were born. Knowing it was a boy helped with the choosing of a name and buying baby clothes.

As well as seeking Andy's input, I wanted Ella, Jo and Leanne to be involved in choosing and agreeing a good name. They rejected some suggestions as there were children they knew at school who they didn't like with that name. Our eventual selection 'Jamie' was chosen by Ella.

I really wanted 'Oliver' as part of the baby's name but then we would have had a 'Jamie Oliver' in the family and I didn't want Jamie named apparently after the TV chef. We all agreed that Jamie was the perfect name and it all felt real once we had the name.

I did however, have some input. At the time I was researching my family tree and what came up regularly on my mum's side was men being called John Wellington Gallant. The latter was my mum's maiden name and so I incorporated this and Jamie would eventually have three middle names. My Uncle John had the same name and my mum was very proud of the name and I felt like I had carried forward a tradition of the family tree.

I often thought Jamie would not like the Wellington part but he loves it. However, from a mum's perspective, I hadn't really anticipated trying to fit such a long name into forms as Jamie grew older!

During this pregnancy I was more aware of the potential diabetic issues and their symptoms but also more aware of what could go wrong.

My pre-natal depression wasn't helped either by the number of balls I was attempting to juggle. There were weekly hospital visits to carry out all the necessary tests. I also didn't want my two teenagers to feel the baby was going to impact the life they were used to so I didn't like to say 'no' to taking them to any of the groups that they attended. And I had a full-time job.

In the second half of this pregnancy I had pre-eclampsia, for which one of the symptoms is high blood pressure. A further symptom was that my feet were very swollen. The weather was getting colder and I struggled with boots and shoes as nothing that I had seemed to fit and walking was difficult.

I was also constantly exhausted but still couldn't sleep. I spent many a night walking around feeling tired but my brain would not shut down. The more I tried to sleep the harder it got. I often would fall asleep just before the alarm went off in the morning and I had to get up to get the children ready for school. I was also working until late on in the pregnancy, so didn't have the option to sleep during the day. This didn't help the depression and I felt my world was caving in. My marriage was going downhill fast. Again I was left feeling unloved.

The baby wasn't due until January 2005 and I did try to keep things as normal as possible for Ella and Jo so they didn't feel they were being pushed out. So for Ella's 13th birthday in November we hired a limousine. This was a great night with Ella and her friends really enjoying it. Little did I know that in only three weeks I was going to give her a brother. We went bowling and to Pizza Hut and it was so nice to see the children happy. It was like a bright star on a very dark night.

I finished work at the beginning of December and then started to get ready for Christmas with the two older children, putting up the Christmas tree etc. I felt like I was nesting and getting ready for the whole baby thing. Baby's clothes were ready and I had bought a pram. It felt strange going back to getting ready for a baby and I often had nightmares that it would all go wrong. This didn't help my sleepless nights.

By now I was going to the hospital daily for monitoring, partly because I was a diabetic and also because the baby's heart traces were not 100 percent. I was offered a place on the hospital ward for rest and to keep an eye on the baby. I was in need of such a rest but decided to decline the offer as, with Andy not being around most of the time, I wanted to be around for my other two children.

Everything seemed to be going okay and then I got a cough and chest infection and then my waters broke, although I didn't realise it at the time.

I thought the extra weight I had gained through the pregnancy plus the coughing was making me wet myself. I also had no experience of waters breaking as my first two babies were delivered via elective Caesarean sections. If I knew what was happening I would have panicked. I was blissfully unaware of the significance of this stage. Even at the daily checks I never mentioned it, believing I had wet myself.

At the next check on Tuesday 7 December, the baby's heart beat was very low and causing concern. There was a discussion over whether to induce the baby there and then. Eventually the doctors decided against this. Instead I was sent home but told to come back later that evening and stay in overnight prior to an elective Caesarean operation in the morning.

So I went home to get my baby bag with all the things I would need and took the two children to my mum's house.

Andy drove me to the hospital and for the first time I felt labour pains. I wasn't sure whether to be excited or scared. I was very worried if the baby would be ok and concerned that my waters had already broken. All I wanted was a healthy baby but as a family we would welcome him with open arms whatever problems he may have.

I needed an emergency Caesarean operation at around 0300 in morning. After my previous two births, this was all quite dramatic, shocking and upsetting. Andy hadn't coped very well and had to leave the hospital before Jamie was born so in those moments, I felt very alone.

Jamie was quickly shown to me. However, he was having breathing difficulties, was quite blue in the face, so they took him straight to the special care unit. Whereas I had been able to hold Ella and Jo before they went to special care, I didn't get to hold Jamie at this point. I was waiting to hear him cry to know he was okay but there were no cries, which made me worry even more.

I next saw Jamie around 5pm later that day in the special care unit but I still couldn't hold him. He ended up being in special care for seven days. I was discharged after five days and then spent the next two days as a stay-in mother on the special care unit until I eventually took him home.

I was torn between being at home for Ella and Jo or staying at the hospital with Jamie. Both Ella and Jo did visit their brother in special care but I still couldn't wait for us all to be together at home.

Going back to the pre-natal depression, the hospital was very aware of the possibility that I might go on and get post-natal depression. Luckily I didn't get any further issues surrounding depression after the birth.

It was like the fog lifted as soon as Jamie was born and I soon started to feel a lot better and was so pleased that this didn't continue into post-natal depression. I made a point of going out for a walk every day and keeping myself healthy by eating well. At last I started sleeping better when I could, fitting rest around looking after a newborn baby and night feeding.

There is one memory that I would like to share from the early weeks of Jamie's life. At Christmas 2004 we went to the nativity play at the church that my parents were heavily involved in. My dad was leading the service and asked if he could borrow his latest grandchild to play a sleeping baby Jesus in the nativity play. When it came to handing him back to me, my dad momentarily forgot his name and so just said, "this is my thirteenth grandchild", and so for a while Jamie was known as "number thirteen" within the family. All the other children in the family were then trying to work out what number they were. So at the next family gathering that Christmas, my children all wanted and were given number badges which represented which number grandchild they were.

I never expected my two older children to assist with caring for Jamie. Ella, who was thirteen and adored him, would bring her school friends home to show them her baby brother. The door would go at 3:30pm and four or five teenage girls would take Jamie to Ella's room and take turns cuddling and holding him. The good thing was that Jamie quickly got used to being passed around and never went through a shy stage.

I loved every moment of having Jamie as a young baby, being a mum again and singing nursery rhymes. I soon joined baby groups and made new friends. He was such a quiet baby and I was glad my little miracle had arrived.

Everyone thought that I was a very happily married woman at this time. However, behind the scenes, my marriage was failing.

MOVING TO BEVERLEY

It was shortly after Jamie's birth that I separated from Andy. He had never come to terms with the fact that I had become pregnant and given birth. I became a single mum again, now with three children, and went to live with my parents whilst I looked for a place to live.

It was a very difficult period of my life. I felt guilty for having another failed marriage although there was nothing I could have done to save it. I did have some very good friends this time and that helped me so much. Having three children all living in one room at my parents' house was difficult, but the support they gave me was amazing.

The four of us moved in with my mum and dad for nearly a month but they never complained once. This support really helped me adjust and once I moved out, I always knew they were only a phone call away. I often called for advice and sometimes just to share my tears.

I found a suitable house for us in Beverley and we moved there in June 2005. The whole house needed decorating from top to bottom and we didn't even have carpets so there was a big task ahead of us. But it was a good time for the children and me and we worked really well as a family, with support from friends.

The two older ones were able to help with painting their own rooms. I must admit I wasn't keen on their colour choice but I allowed them to use their artistic flair.

Even the large garden needed plenty doing to it and a local charity helped with this so we had an area for the three children to play. We had a few barbeques that year to say 'thank you' to all of our friends, new ones and old ones. We made a really good start in Beverley. Our situation wasn't ideal but we made the best of what we had. It's in difficult times you find who your friends are and also make new ones.

Ella and Jo changed schools, made new friends very quickly and did very well in their new schools. In fact the school move turned out to be very good for them, especially Ella, and they both enjoyed it more than their previous school. It helped me knowing they were happy and that I had made the right choice by moving them.

I encouraged them to bring friends home and the house soon became full of life just like it was as I was growing up. I liked the fact that I had an open door policy and people felt free to drop by for a cup of tea and a chat.

I made friends in the street and found that we had a lovely elderly couple next door and generally really nice neighbours who were quick to help out. Several popped round on the day we moved in with offers of assistance and information which made for a very warm welcome.

One thing I found strange in the early days was on a number of occasions, men that I didn't know would knock at my door. The first time it happened the man spoke very little English but I worked out that he was offering me money. I just sent him away saying he must have the wrong house. This happened a few times and it was baffling me as to what it was all about. One day I mentioned it to a friend whom I had made in our street. She laughed and explained that the lady who owned the house before me allegedly had a dubious reputation for welcoming these male visitors. It turned out that these were servicemen from other countries training at a local RAF base. I threatened them with police involvement and also rang the base directly and spoke to someone senior. The visits ceased immediately.

One of the things I hoped to find more time to do as we settled into life in Beverley was photography. I had a long-standing interest in this hobby since being a child and working out what was a good picture and what wasn't came very naturally to me.

To supplement my natural ability, I had previously undertaken two years of evening class lessons, completing stage 1 and stage 2 in photography. I really wanted to put it all into practice in such a beautiful town where there were lots of buildings and views of interest to a photographer. Everywhere you looked, there was a photo opportunity in Beverley. It is such a beautiful town and well worth a visit.

Photography had also moved into the digital age where you could take as many pictures as you wanted. I had already done some wedding photography for friends. After one wedding photo-shoot, my pictures were used by the bride and groom instead of the official photographs as the latter didn't come out as well as expected.

I was really keen to find the time for my hobby in and around Beverley. I had plenty of ideas for photography projects and it was a case of 'one day I will go and do this'. However, the reality was that I was a mum with a young baby and two teenagers who came first. The photography projects kept being put to one side and 'one day' never arrived.

I always thought that I would have plenty of time to pursue my hobby in and around Beverley. Little did I know that my sight loss would stop me.

This period also saw the number of family pets increase. We had brought an old ginger tom with us and we got another cat so that when ginger tom died the children would not be upset. Of course ginger tom outlived the other cat and two other cats that we subsequently got. He was a firm favourite in the street and people would often stop to stroke him.

Jo especially wanted a dog and it was a time when we could fit a dog into our lifestyle. So along came 'Bob', a black Labrador who we saw advertised on a website for dogs needing new homes. His previous owner was moving to Australia and sadly for her was unable to take Bob overseas to her new home. She was very pleased when Jo and Bob immediately became great friends. Bob loved nothing more than to chase a ball around the garden and so with two energetic teenagers to play with, he had the perfect life. Bob's very tolerant and loving nature quickly meant that he became a firm family favourite.

With Beverley being very close to the East Yorkshire countryside there were lots of scenic dog walks nearby. In particular, we all enjoyed walks onto the Westwood at Beverley, a big open space within walking distance of the town centre. There was usually an ice cream van there too and we often stopped for a treat before heading home.

We also used to walk along Beverley Beck. We quickly discovered that as soon as Bob saw water he thought, 'ah lovely water for Bob to jump in' regardless of how deep the water was and so we had to keep him on a lead unless we wanted to take a very wet dog home.

Bob also enjoyed our regular trips to Hornsea, a seaside town only half an hour away. We would walk along the seafront and he was allowed to jump in the sea. We would then all have fish and chip suppers before driving home. It was great sharing these times with the children and Bob. These remain great memories for me that nobody can take away. Looking back, this period was a really lovely time, especially as we were all smiling again. It was great to hear all of my children laughing.

I always encouraged the children to be involved in lots of different clubs and out of school activities. They had joined some of the clubs whilst we lived in Hull and I was happy for both Ella and Jo to continue to go to these. They also kept friendships from Hull with my blessing. As Hull is ten miles from Beverley, this did mean that 'mum's taxi' could be very busy as I took the children to and from activities. I didn't mind this at all; it was my way of being a mum. I also didn't want my children on street corners just hanging around. I felt it was important that I took them to youth groups and different clubs and encouraged them to meet new friends and have new experiences. They also used Facebook Messenger to keep in touch with friends from their previous school and their social lives were far busier than my own.

I had decided that after two failed marriages that Ella and Jo deserved my undivided attention and I wouldn't seek another serious relationship until after they had both left home and gone to university. And of course I was also too busy looking after the children to go out and look for a relationship. Given my past history, I also needed time to heal and this worked very well for us all.

So far I haven't mentioned my diabetes during this chapter. Having a strict diabetic routine such as regular mealtimes was sometimes difficult to achieve when you have three children to look after. So looking after myself sometimes took second place. In hindsight I should have looked after my diabetes better and avoided any unintended impact on my children. In due course when I contracted meningitis it was during a period when my diabetes was not being well-controlled. This made me more susceptible to such illnesses and the subsequent recovery a lot slower.

It was probably because I had become complacent. I felt that I knew it all and had read everything about diabetes. I was too busy running around and doing things and I forgot the basics.

I admit that I avoided going to my hospital appointments, thinking I knew everything and that there was nothing new they could do for me. And they didn't know how hard it was being a single mum. So it would be a waste of time.

I would let my blood sugar levels run too high on too many occasions because I didn't want the condition to take over and control my life. You can't hide from it and basically I put my head in the sand about how much the diabetes was affecting my body. This meant that I had a hand in my subsequent health issues.

Whilst it's too late for me now, the learning point here is never overlook the need to control your diabetes. Good control will help avoid further complications, as I was to find out in the not too distant future.

MENINGITIS

If you Google my name, you can read articles about my sight loss, often squashed into a one or two-page article.

Being interviewed for these articles was an important part of my life and gave me the idea about working with the media and helping others.

As a result of articles about me appearing in magazines such as 'Woman's Weekly' many people contacted me saying that my story was inspirational. At last the cloud had a silver lining - I could help others.

After seeing how my story was helping others, I started to think about writing this book.

There wasn't room in the magazine articles to tell the whole of my sight loss story. I won't be glossing over any details in what follows, however shocking or upsetting. There is also humour along the way.

Nobody thinks sight loss will happen to them. I never thought it would happen to me, even after being diabetic since age 13.

I was now a mother of three children – two teenagers and a toddler. As I've described, I love all my children and they are my world. So for a mother, the hardest thing about sight loss is knowing how much this will change their lives forever. I certainly never wanted my sight loss to mean they would become my carers.

I wanted from day one to protect my children from my sight loss as much as possible. I wanted them to feel normal in school, and avoid the issues I had to deal with in my own schooldays.

I think this stems back to a moment in my school life when a mother of a girl in my school came in to talk about being a guide dog owner. I felt so sorry for this girl, who was called Julia and was aged about ten, that I gave her my sweets one break time.

Before I move on and try and tell you about how my sight loss journey began, I need to talk about my sister Michelle. She was fostered by my parents and came and joined our family at a very young age. Michelle had a fair few health problems, including being totally blind. As I was brought up with Michelle, we shared a bedroom along with my other sisters. As a child I never saw Michelle as blind, I just saw her as my sister 'Shelly' and this is still the case today.

This made my own sight loss easier to handle. I knew I was Dianne: mother, sister, child and friend. I'm not blind Dianne, I am DIANNE.

April 2007 was the beginning of my sight loss story although I didn't know it at the time. It started as a normal Saturday morning. I had driven 12 miles to take Jo to a club he attended (he had just turned 13). It was a difficult drive as I had a painful headache, which I put down to being a busy mum. Having dropped Jo off, I started to drive back. Although my head was getting worse I thought nothing about it. I came to the conclusion that it was a migraine, especially as the lights from other cars seemed to be making it worse.

When I arrived back home the pain was so bad I just wanted to take some painkillers and sleep in a dark room. I felt very cold and was shivering. I failed to notice that my temperature was very high.

I am not sure if it was the pain preventing my brain from working or the fact I did have meningitis. Thinking back, if my children had any of these symptoms I would have suspected meningitis and taken them straight to the hospital. However, I didn't seek help.

I laid Jamie down in his cot for his routine sleep. Ella, who was now 16, loved reading and as usual had her head in a book. I knocked on her bedroom door to let her know that I had a bit of a headache and was going to have a nap while Jamie was asleep and to wake me if she needed anything.

I then closed the curtains, curled up on the sofa in the front room, and wrapped myself in a big heavy quilt that I brought downstairs from my bedroom. I was relieved that I could shut my eyes and sleep, thinking that after some painkillers and a catnap I would be back to normal and be able to collect Jo.

It was just so nice to shut my eyes believing it would all be ok in half an hour. How wrong I was!

Ella later came downstairs and realised that I hadn't woken as expected and I needed to go and collect Jo. She tried to wake me up and, getting no response, went to fetch a neighbour and also rang my mum, who immediately came across.

The neighbour contacted the on-call doctor but there was a delay in the doctor being able to attend. Once my mum arrived thirty minutes after getting the call from Ella, she insisted that they call an ambulance straightaway.

I remember hearing Ella, my neighbour and my mum speaking – were they in the room or was it part of my dream? Everything seemed really foggy. I seemed to lose track of time and couldn't seem to wake up. The dream was turning into some sort of nightmare.

By this time, my GP had arrived followed soon after by an ambulance.

I remember thinking, 'please can somebody tell me what's going on'? Different people started to speak. My head felt like it was going to burst. What was going on? I realised that I was very scared.

Then everything went quiet and peaceful. As I drifted into deeper unconsciousness, the pain disappeared and I was sat in a green field enjoying the sun. It felt so nice.

Then I was back to where everybody was talking and tapping my face. "Come on Dianne, we need you to wake up." My eyes were too heavy to open but I could hear the people. I wanted to tell my mum I was ok but it was all so strange. I wanted to go back to the peaceful field. I remember being given an injection and my mum crying and saying something about meningitis. But I could not really understand it. I drifted back to my field and peace with no pain.

It was decided that I needed to go straight to hospital as an emergency case and my mum came with me, leaving the children to be looked after by neighbours.

I must have suddenly panicked about my children. Whilst we were in the ambulance rushing to the hospital, I briefly regained consciousness. I don't remember this moment, but my mum said that I told her very clearly that I wanted her to make sure the children were looked after.

I then shut my eyes and went back to the green field and sunshine.

I was taken immediately to the resuscitation unit where a team of doctors started to work on me. They did some scans of my brain and these revealed that fortunately there had been no bleeds in my brain. Within the hour, a spinal tap revealed that I did indeed have meningitis.

I was put into an isolation room with all the medical staff having to wear masks and gowns to prevent the risk of infection being passed on. It was later confirmed that my meningitis was viral in nature rather than bacterial and so it wasn't contagious. I was in hospital for a week and received antibiotics by a drip to help me recover. I felt very weak and couldn't even find the energy to sit up in bed. I was in a lot of pain and couldn't concentrate for long enough to think about even the simple things in life.

As I was not able to take decisions about who should look after my children, my parents took the lead and all three children went to stay with them.

After three or four days I started to feel restless and requested to go home. This seemed the best way to put the incident behind me and get back to normal life.

After a week in hospital, I was allowed out to rest at home. My parents gave me the option of not having the children back immediately but I wanted them to come home and get back to normality at the earliest opportunity. Whilst I should really have been resting with my feet up, the reality was that I went back to being a normal mum almost straightaway.

Three to four weeks later, I was contacted by Meningitis UK who provided details of a helpline to use if I felt that I needed to talk with anybody. Whilst I didn't take up the offer of counselling, I did find their website very informative. Subsequently I agreed to feature in an article for a daily newspaper on meningitis to raise awareness of early symptoms of adult meningitis as it is often wrongly assumed that this potentially fatal illness only affects children.

SIGHT LOSS

Four months after having meningitis, I woke up one morning to find that overnight, and without any warning, I had lost my sight. I will never forget the date – 26 August 2007. Life would never be the same again.

Since having meningitis, I had noticed that my sight had deteriorated. Indeed, very recently I had been to the opticians for a sight test and had ended up paying quite a lot of money for a very nice pair of glasses, which I never actually got to use. Nothing was picked up when my eyes were checked at the optician's.

No one was aware that my sight loss was going to happen and it couldn't have been detected without an examination of the back of the eyes using dilation drops.

I had assumed the change to my vision was an age thing rather than a medical condition. However, I found out later that having the meningitis had really affected my diabetes and there were lots of diabetic issues going on. These ultimately led to a severe bleed going on behind my eye.

I had kept putting off going to the hospital as I was a busy working mother and the thought of having drops put in my eyes didn't appeal. And I would then need to arrange to get a lift home after having dilation drops. It all seemed so much to deal with and at the time, not important.

But in layman's terms what was happening to me was that the tiny blood vessels in the back of my eye, which we all have, had grown until they eventually burst. The blood from the burst covered my vision field leaving just tiny areas to view through. This made my vision cloudy because it was happening behind my eye.

My eyes still look the same so people often say, 'you don't look blind'. But I do find that bright lights, sunny days and camera flashes make my eyes squint. On photographs I often now have half-closed eyes.

I am now wiser as a result and advise people that if they are diabetic and are having sight issues then it doesn't take long to go to your GP or the hospital and get it checked it out.

You never know what is going on behind your eyes. If this book convinces everybody reading it to go to eye appointments, then I'm sure it will save somebody's sight. You can't afford to ignore eye appointments. I found out being able to see was something I took for granted.

As I was saying, it was the August Bank Holiday. I was spending the weekend in the house with my three children. The Saturday night had been a quiet evening in and I had an early night. On the Sunday I had planned to take Ella and Jo out in the car. We had a family evening in with a takeaway as a treat and I watched a film with the children. Little did I know this was my last evening as a sighted person. What would have been on my 'sight loss bucket list' if I had written one? What would be on your list?

When I woke up on the Sunday morning I realised straightaway that something was wrong. I couldn't see anything with my right eye and there were lots of floating bits in my left eye which blurred my vision. I kept shutting and opening them, expecting it to be different each time that I opened them. My brain couldn't seem to understand that I couldn't see. I just assumed that it was just something that was going to go away. I wasn't scared initially as I thought it was just a short-term problem and nothing to worry about.

It seems I had a pattern when it came to dealing with an unexpected problem; leave it and it will go away.

On my way to the bathroom, I kept walking into things, especially on the right side. In the bathroom I generally felt disorientated, a little bit like when you are drunk. Only this time I was perfectly sober.

I washed my face with cold water as I tried to get my eyes to wake up. But it just didn't happen. I then looked in the mirror but for the first time ever, I could not see myself looking back. This was a strange sensation and I even tried to clean the mirror, as though there was condensation on it, but this didn't help either.

I started to realise that this wasn't going to just go away and a sense of fear, shock and deep down sickness took over. I started to panic and could feel my heart pounding as I wondered, "what am I going to do". It is very difficult looking back to explain just how much this was affecting me and all I can say is that I have never known panic like it since.

I went to check that Ella was up and, after exchanging the usual morning pleasantries, told her that I was having difficulty seeing that morning and that, as I wouldn't be able to drive, I would have to get someone else to take her and her brother out. Her response was, "what do you mean you can't see!"

I told her not to worry about it, thinking that once I'd eaten breakfast everything would somehow be all right. Silently I was wishing, 'please let this be just a temporary blip', and started to wonder how I would tell two young teenagers that their mum was going blind?

I then rang my parents and told my mum I couldn't see anything out of my right eye and that the vision in my left eye was cloudy and not the way it should be. I recall that I was very calm throughout but I could tell that Mum was very worried.

I played it down as it would have hurt me to know that I had upset her. I also knew that if I broke down talking to my mum that I would lose control and the crying would never stop. Also I thought that if I cried and let it all out then it would mean that I was accepting that it was happening.

Even then I didn't go to hospital until later in the day as I had decided to wait until midday to see if my sight came back. I'm not sure what I was expecting to happen. I also felt that I would be wasting NHS time. They had adverts asking people not to turn up at A&E if it wasn't an emergency. As I wasn't going to die if I didn't go, I didn't see it as an emergency.

During the morning I rang a friend, Joanne, and told her what had happened and that I might need to go to the hospital. Straightaway she offered to take me. Midday arrived and there was no change in my sight. However, I didn't feel ill, except that my eyes were struggling. I certainly didn't want to turn up at hospital only to find that the problem had resolved itself, although maybe that was wishful thinking on my part.

Joanne then got me to ring the Eye Hospital (part of Hull Royal Infirmary) and explain what had happened to me. They told me to come straight in to them rather than go to A&E first and so Joanne kindly gave me a lift. This made me worry. My heart was pounding with nervous anticipation and worry, admitting it was happening.

I only waited five or ten minutes before I got to see a doctor. He sat me on a chair, covered my left eye and asked me to read one of those boards with letters on used during sight tests. Unfortunately, I couldn't even see where the board was. This really hit me and I got quite upset that I couldn't see it. My first realisation was, 'this isn't good'.

After more checks, the doctor explained to me that I'd had a really big bleed in my eye and he wasn't sure what they could do about it and didn't know whether they could operate and sort it out. He arranged for me to see a consultant on the Tuesday morning, the 28th August.

At that stage, and indeed for the first year, I still hoped it would be resolved. Maybe somewhere around the corner they would discover a cure that could be used on me. I watched the news thinking a cure for blindness would be found. In fact many people's reaction in the early days was that, 'medical science is amazing and things are improving and cures found all the time'. I understood, as that would be my way to comfort people if the shoe was on the other foot.

We went home and I realised at that stage that I couldn't even make a cup of tea. My friend stayed with me for a while but she did have her own family to look after so she eventually went home that evening. Later, Ella, Jo and Jamie came home as planned. I didn't want them to stay with my mum because if I told them that I couldn't look after them because of my sight loss they would be so worried. Right from day one I wanted the impact on them to be as minimal as possible. As I wasn't up to cooking tea, we had a takeaway. Even though Ella and Jo were old enough to help in the house, I remember feeling very scared and isolated.

During that day I had encountered every raw emotion going. I was desperate to go to bed that night as it meant that I could shut my eyes and pretend that I could see. And for the first few weeks I used to dream as a sighted person. When you go to sleep you are just the same as everyone else. This became my escape.

In the following days my GP and a Health Visitor got involved. This scared me and I thought, "will they take my children away if I can't manage?"

So on top of sight loss I had a bigger worry - what happens to children in this situation. This was all new to me. I couldn't even match socks anymore, how would I manage taking care of my three beautiful children. How could I make it right for them?

My mum moved in to stay with us for two weeks. The good thing was that she allowed me to be as independent as possible, encouraging me to take on challenges as they came along. She made me carry on and so there was no time for staying in bed feeling sorry for myself. As a mum myself, I can understand how hard it must have been to stand back and watch me struggling. But Mum was helping me come to terms with the challenges that I had to face and this made me stronger.

I was fortunate to have a good circle of friends too, and in the first few weeks, people would bring meals around such as pasta bakes. I realise that I was lucky to have such a good set of friends. Thanks to you all for your help in those early days.

The hardest thing was that my youngest Jamie hadn't yet learned to talk due to learning issues. I asked the Health Visitor for advice and how to work out where he was. Her response was that she had heard that blind people but bells on young children so they'd know where they were. I dismissed the idea telling her that he was not a dog and I wasn't going to do that. Little did I know this was going to be a great way to track my lovely toddler.

It helped so much when I started meeting other visually-impaired (VI) mums as I often felt that although the professionals were trying to help, they did not fully understand as they had never been in the same situation.

So later on when I met a VI who actually did attach a bell to her young daughter, I immediately accepted it as a good idea as it was from another VI mum. Meeting others in the same situation is the best way to move forward. It's reassuring and inspirational.

All the time, I was aware that my sight wasn't improving. I had extensive laser treatment under a general anaesthetic in the intervening period to try and improve my eyesight but whilst it had stopped the left side getting worse, it hadn't brought about the improvement that I had been hoping for.

Six weeks after my vision deteriorated, and just after my 39th birthday, I was formally told that that my sight loss was indeed permanent. I think that I was still living in shock from August 26.

I had an appointment in early October with the consultant for a review after the laser treatment. The clinic was very busy and was over-running. I was one of last appointments and was told by the consultant, in a matter of fact way, that there was no further treatment available in my case. My world and my only hope all came crashing down. The shock I felt on this day was like when I lost my sight, but now the only hope that was keeping me going had been taken away.

I felt very angry. I was told to come back in two weeks and they would add my details to the blind register. I left the consulting room and was in tears in the corridor. As the clinic was shutting and the nurses were packing away, there was no one I could talk to.

I wanted to shout at the staff, 'can't you see today I feel like my life has ended and you all carry on is if nothing was happening'? To be fair, they had no idea what the consultant had told me.

This was before the days when there were Eye Clinic Liaison Officers, or ECLOs, available who are dedicated support workers for newly visually impaired people. Subsequently, I have fought to ensure that every hospital in the UK has an ECLO. They are one of the most important people in the eye clinic when you have been informed that you have sight issues and can help you get registered with the relevant authorities, put you in touch with local support groups and generally provide a light at the end of a very dark tunnel.

As there was no counsellor available, my friend suggested, 'let's go for food and we'll get a few glasses of wine into you'. I guess doing something normal helped me to adjust to the news, although I can't say the wine made it any easier to accept what I had just been told.

Over the next few days, with the help of friends and family, I joined a 'Google group' for newly Visually Impaired people. These were the days before Facebook Groups. However, I struggled to use the computer at this stage. I didn't have any specialist software and didn't know how to magnify things on the screen. I also used to get lots of headaches.

It helped that people from the VI support group that I had joined started to contact me. They would telephone me and let me talk about my concerns and so on. One in particular remains a very good friend to this day. I couldn't have managed without these people in my early days.

At this point, I would like to formally record my gratitude to anybody working on a helpline or in a sight loss support group such as the people who assisted me. You are very important and make all the difference.

Obviously I wasn't able to work – no one wants blood taken by a blind person. I was signed off sick and unfortunately was never able to return to my nursing job that I loved so much. I wanted to be the care giver not receiver.

Something else that was very difficult was my car. It was still on the drive. It was like the elephant in the room that no one wanted to talk about. Indeed, one neighbour was heard to say that I could not possibly be blind as I still had a car. When I eventually got rid of the car, it was like saying 'goodbye' to a part of me and more significantly, a big part of my independence.

My mum asked me what I was going to do now. My reply to her was that I was going to abseil off the Humber Bridge for charity. This was a sign of things to come. When I fight back, I really fight back.

I was very determined that my children would not become my carers. I looked into getting rehabilitation support. However, there were not many rehab workers specialising in VI people available in my area. This was vital as they could show me how to undertake household chores and how to make a cup of tea without burning myself.

There was a three month waiting list. I couldn't wait for that amount of time as I was a mother with three children and didn't feel that my situation could wait three months, so I eventually contacted my local MP to fight my case.

My aim was to be independent. I wanted to be able to go out to the local shop and back on my own, without waiting for somebody to come and take me. I wanted to be able to go out on my own for a cup of coffee and then come back again.

Whilst I was sometimes depressed, my over-whelming desire was to ensure that my sight loss affected my children as little as possible, which I think is what any mother would do.

My upbringing also helped. My parents were practising Christians and I was brought up with the belief that everything happens for the good and God would not let you suffer more than you can take. God must have thought I was a strong person as I must admit at the time, I felt I was drowning. Having that sort of upbringing made me look at the brighter side of life. Indeed, I would like the song, 'Always Look on the Bright Side of Life' to be played at my funeral.

And yes, maybe deep down I was hoping for a cure. I think anyone in a similar situation would.

However, I now know that if I could cure one thing —sight loss or diabetes — I would choose for the world to be free of diabetes. My reasoning is that over the years I have managed to adjust to my sight loss. As an example, I only had a shower fitted after my sight loss so I never needed to relearn how to use it once I became VI. Would I understand how to use it if one day a miracle happened and I could see the shower? I am sure I would have to close my eyes to use it. I hope you can understand what I am saying.

FIRST YEAR OF BEING VI

The first few weeks of being blind/visually impaired (VI) were very difficult. But I needed to move on and learn how to live with it.

Firstly, I need to explain whether I saw myself as blind or visually impaired (VI). On my certificate of visual impairment, I was classed as 'severely visually impaired (blind)'. The lesser option would have been, 'partial visual impairment'. I found this confusing. My sister was totally blind whilst I still had a little bit of sight. But we were both in the same category of visual impairment.

The limited vision I was left with in late 2007 is pretty much what I still have today. I am completely blind in my right eye although I do have some limited vision (approximately 5 percent) in my left.

The best way to describe it is to imagine looking through a sieve – there are six small holes that I look through. I also have black floating things that can obscure my vision. Over the time I have learned to use my limited vision to its full extent although at first it was so unusual and so difficult that I couldn't use it.

Right from the start, people would ask me about my sight. It has always been difficult to explain in straightforward terms. It is worth bearing in mind here that only 5 percent of people registered blind are totally blind. People would just ask in the street, 'are you really blind'? which I found offensive. I would never stop a person in a wheelchair and ask, 'what are you doing in that wheelchair, why are you in it'? I do find it very rude when strangers ask for details about my sight. From talking to other VI people, it isn't just me that it has happened to. This seems to be a fairly common occurrence.

But, let's go back to my first year of being VI. After the first few weeks, life became more settled. My mum moved back to her house and people stopped sending cooked meals. So I needed to start thinking about life and how to move forward. I guess it started to sink in that this was not going away. I had to learn to relive my life as a VI person. Things were going to change and I had to accept that this was happening day in, day out. Inside I was screaming but I wanted to make life as easy as possible for my family and friends. I think at times I was a good actress.

I can understand why people struggle with sight loss and don't leave the house for years. I think if I had been aware of the RNIB's emotional support service I would have had a chat with them. The beauty about talking about your fears with a support service such as the RNIB's is that they understand your situation and that's why they are there. Some of the people handling calls are VI themselves. You don't need to worry about speaking out, upsetting family and friends. So if you are in this situation, please call the RNIB emotional support service. A problem shared is a problem halved. Please see the notes at end of this book on how to contact the RNIB.

I realised that whatever frustrations I had needed to be channelled into taking positive steps and get on with life. I guess my inner determination was once again showing up.

I was constantly chasing the rehab service for the help that I felt I needed to become self-sufficient. But I was struggling to even get an appointment. Eventually I rang my MP Graham Stuart who was really helpful. Indeed, within two days the rehab services had arranged an appointment with me.

I have subsequently worked with Graham on a number of campaigns on VI issues and am still actively involved in resolving issues with the local rehab services today.

Chrissie, the rehab worker who was eventually assigned to my case, spent a lot of time with me in those early days. She was a very down to earth person and often went above and beyond the call of duty and would fit me in between other calls.

I then had to face my first Christmas, 2007, as a VI mother. I remember that a friend gave me and the children a lift to York so we could visit the Christmas market there. It was really busy and I was also just learning to use a long white cane. Because the streets were so busy, not everyone could see that I was using a cane although on this particular day I was finding this difficult to come to terms with. At one point I got really cross and frustrated and stormed off. Without realising it, I walked through the middle of the Salvation Army brass band that was getting ready to play, much to the amusement of my children.

When it came to presents, I was determined to buy presents for my children myself but of course there was no online shopping then. The hardest part was knowing which presents were for which child and keeping track of how many I had bought for each as I wanted to ensure that each of my children received a fair amount. The best way I found to achieve this was to use different coloured wrapping paper for each child.

However, I didn't send any Christmas cards which I felt quite guilty about, but writing was nearly impossible. I thought about buying braille cards but nobody would be able to read them.

Shopping was getting harder as the nearer we got to Christmas, the busier the shops became. Also the days got darker earlier and, as my night vision is very limited, this was when I felt the most vulnerable. In particular, I found that bright car lights in a dark street to be very disorientating.

Eating out became a bit of a challenge as it takes courage to say that you can't read a menu in a restaurant or pub and ask for assistance. For a while I always ordered fish and chips but in the end I got bored with always having the same meal. I discovered that checking the menu online beforehand often worked, otherwise I put my pride to one side and simply asked for help. And everybody I have ever asked to read a menu to me has been happy to do so and indeed they often tell me much more about individual dishes, and which are the most popular. From their point of view, they don't want to cause offence by offering to read the menu to a VI person, so it is up to me to say when I need help. It's as simple as that.

My parents had offered to do Christmas lunch and that we could spend Christmas Day with them. However, I decided to be independent and do it myself at my own house. To practice, I cooked a Sunday roast a few weeks before Christmas. I got everything set out and went to the freezer and got out what I thought were frozen Yorkshire puddings.

It turned out that these were frozen scones, which the children obviously spotted when I put the meal out. So I quickly said the meal was sweet and sour chicken! I found it best to be humorous with the children when I made mistakes cooking and we shared a number of jokes about my mishaps in the kitchen. I preferred to do it this way rather than sit back and tell the two older children that they would have to cook for me. I am also a woman of great humour.

I found that I needed to be careful with 'best before dates' on foods and ensure I was not giving the children out of date food. You soon realise when you are eating an out of date yoghurt. At moments like this, life can be very frustrating.

It was clear that I needed some help and as I didn't want my children to have to be my carers, I realised this would mean people coming in to the house to initially help me and observe how I would manage with preparing meals, household chores and childcare. I had a big fight with Social Services to get the help I needed. It's also hard to admit you need help. To others reading this in a similar situation, I would just say that asking for help doesn't mean you are weak.

Another problem that I had not anticipated appeared in January - ice and snow. Ice, and in particular black ice, is very hard to walk on when using a cane and snow makes it difficult to work out where the path ends and the road begins. To help me, I bought a good pair of boots with lots of grip but on some days I decided that it would not be safe for me to go out and instead I accepted help from others if I needed something fetching from the local shop.

Over the first few months, whoever was available from the Social Services' carers would come in. This made it really difficult for me. Every time I had to explain how things ran in the house and where things were. They would then leave and I would not be able to find where they had put things.

It became easier once my own care package was agreed and I could employ people myself. The first person I employed just before Christmas 2007 was my niece, Claire. She was someone I knew and trusted and she was absolutely amazing.

I also had to come to terms with not having a job. Going back to work wasn't an option and I didn't want to go on sickness benefit because in my mind I was capable of working. However, I didn't know what job I would be able to do. I wanted to prove that I had a brain and I was still a person so initially I went onto income support.

At this stage family holidays were not really an option. Our last holiday had been in August 2007 when we went to Seahouses in Northumberland, the week before I lost my sight.

Early on, I decided that doing an Open University Course was something that I could do. I contacted the Open University and they did an assessment. I was delighted to be accepted onto an English Literature course, covering authors such as Jane Austen, run by St John's College at York.

The Open University were very supportive. They provided me with an upgraded computer with 'Jaws' software, which read out words as they appeared on the screen such as emails and articles, and bought special lighting to help me work on the computer at home. They even provided me with a dicta-phone to record lectures and paid for someone to attend lectures with me and help me take notes.

I had also been in contact with the Royal National Institute of Blind People (RNIB) and they gave me access to their talking book service. This gave help with both university books and books I read for pleasure, which is something I continue to enjoy to this day.

And I was still a mum to a toddler. Jamie had just started at nursery and whilst the education department provided transport to take us both to the nursery, I had to make my own way back home. With the assistance of the rehab worker, I had taught myself this route.

One day I came out of the nursery and a lady, trying to be helpful, took me across the road even though I hadn't asked. Unfortunately, as I had worked out the route so precisely from the nursery door, I panicked and was then completely disorientated even though I had lived in Beverley for two years. I remember been scared and as I couldn't see a street name, I couldn't even ring a taxi to help me home.

Even today I am always grateful when people offer assistance but please do check first that the blind person does need assistance before taking them across the road!

A funny thing once happened to me when I was waiting with my white cane for my two teenagers outside a supermarket. An elderly gentleman came up to me and put some coins in my hand and said, "This is for the blind." I was so shocked that he had walked away before I had a chance to explain that I wasn't collecting for a blind charity. When my teenagers returned, they both found it extremely funny. The money went to a good cause as I put it into a Guide Dogs' collection box.

I made a mental note to myself not to leave my white cane lying around in case my eldest son Jo decided it would be a good game to stand outside shops with a cane collecting money.

Jo found that having a VI mum came with certain benefits. He wasn't keen on school PE lessons and so decided to use one of my electricity bills, that was written in braille, as a 'letter from mum' excusing him from PE. As the teachers could not read braille they were none the wiser. He carried this off for three years until his PE teacher stopped me at a school open night and said, "I would have liked to have been able to read those letters that you have been sending me for the last three years." I guess that was what you call, 'thinking outside of the box'.

I wanted the opportunity to meet other VI people. Social Services did offer me the opportunity of regular visits to a day centre at the local Blind Institute. I didn't feel it was appropriate for me as the other people there would have been older than me and I didn't want to do basket weaving and play blind bingo.

What happened instead was that I started to meet other VI people who I had met via Google Groups. By now, my computer had the necessary software which made it easy for me to chat online all night from my own home with other VI people. This was very helpful learning from others in the same situation.

Through these chats I found out that there was a Goalball group in the Hull and East Yorkshire area. Goalball is a form of football for VI people. On the first night somebody dropped me off at the place where the Goalball group met and I was left on my own. At first I felt really scared but this soon changed when I realised that I was in a group of people who were having a laugh and a normal evening. I was also meeting other VI people who were as determined as me. I was laughing and smiling again.

For first time ever I was with VI people in the same age group as me. I was so ecstatic at meeting other VI people who embraced being VI that I couldn't get to sleep that night.

I kept the Goalball up and eventually represented my team at intermediate group level. My daughter and her partner also became volunteers at the group.

I found that playing Goalball, where all players wear blackout goggles and have to listen for the bells in a ball that can be coming in your direction at great speed, gave me orientation skills. This helped me move around in traffic a lot easier.

Eventually I retired from Goalball as I had broken some bones and lost a tooth whilst playing. However, it was still a good point in my life. I have the medals to prove it.

As my first year of being VI came to a close, I felt as though I had achieved so much. I had wanted to do it for my children. I had wanted my parents to see that I could manage.

My confidence was growing, I was proving to myself and others that I could cope and wasn't afraid to try different things.

But there were difficult moments as well. I remember that around this time, somebody came into the front garden and started to smash our lights. However, I realised that I couldn't see enough of their features to describe them if I had called the police. This not only spoilt the look of my garden, but was an issue as the lights had been placed in the garden to help me at night. At times like this you become vulnerable and scared in your own home. I suppose the teenagers doing this kind of thing think it is just a bit of a laugh. However, the effect on the victims can last for the rest of their lives.

My experiences made me realise that there was a real need for more local support for VI people. Eventually this led to me starting the charity – VisAbility.

I also realised that having a guide dog would be really beneficial and help me get more out of life.

It took me a while but eventually I was beginning to get my independence back. It was a different life but it was a good life and my humour was coming back. Life's too short not to smile.

GUIDE DOGS AND HATTIE

Prior to my own sight loss, if I passed a guide dog collection I would think 'cute clever dog, poor blind person'. I would put my loose change into the box and that was my bit done.

Very early on in my sight loss journey, I knew I wanted to have a guide dog. But I was unsure how you went about it. I must admit in my mind it was a bit like collecting a rescue dog. You popped to the kennels and chose a dog you liked. Then it looks after you.

So, I found the number for my local Guide Dogs for the Blind Association office and rang them to request a dog. Little did I know there was, and still is, a two year waiting list. I made the call and a few days later I had my first visit from a Guide Dogs' representative.

It was still early days but talking with Alison gave me hope that my independence had a chance to come back. The moment I realised that a dog could become my helper, then I felt that I had made the first step of the journey to more independence.

Guide Dogs was happy for me to apply. One thing I was unsure of was whether only totally blind people can have a guide dog. The answer was that if a dog gives you independence and you have some degree of sight loss then you will be considered.

The first time I walked with a guide dog was completely unexpected. I was at a sight exhibition organised by a local blind charity.

Guide Dogs had a stand and I went over to see the people on the stand (well, the dogs really). I met a yellow Labrador cross retriever called Hattie. She was very excitable, which was not what I expected from a guide dog. Then I was asked, "Would you like to have a try walking her in a harness?"

This question was music to my ears and I immediately replied, "Yes please!"

I was a bit nervous when we went outside as it was time to hand over my white cane and try walking with a dog. Indeed, the moment you put your trust in a dog is very strange. I listened to the instructor and off we went. With the help of the instructor, I gave Hattie her instructions. My first guide dog walk, and my first walk to freedom.

At the end of the walk I was told I did well. The disappointing news was that Hattie was already paired with a lady. My wait for a dog went on. That night was the first time that in my dreams I was visually impaired, and I dreamt that I was working with Hattie.

I continued working hard with the Guide Dogs' mobility team and my rehab worker to gain the skills I needed as a cane and guide dog owner.

As an example I was taught how to use a pedestrian crossing safely. Obviously, a guide dog cannot understand that the green man on the pedestrian lights means it is safe to cross. But a VI person still needs to be able to cross safely. But how? Well, on the box with the wait button is a cone underneath and this spins around as long as the green man is on and it is safe to cross. Amazingly, I never knew this. Now I will make one request. Please don't let anyone put bubble gum on it. It's not a good experience for visually impaired people.

A few weeks passed and then THE call came! Guide Dogs wanted to visit the next day. The person on the phone told me that Hattie and her new owner unfortunately hadn't made a good match. So they would like to see if Hattie would be a good match for me. I put the phone down and cried, but this time they were tears of joy. At last I had good news for the children.

Guide Dogs arranged for two weeks of intense training from my home for Hattie and me to see if we were going to be a working team. Guide Dogs also wanted to gradually introduce Hattie to Bob, our pet dog, so that Bob would welcome this new dog and share his territory at home with her.

In preparation, I went to the pet shop to get pink toys, a bed and bowls for food and water – the works! The lady at the till said, "It's a girl then!"

Hattie was going to join our family as our newest member. And it was the start of a new chapter in my life.

Those two weeks training were very hard work for both Hattie and me. A few moments from that time stand out for me. Firstly, you no longer have use of the cane, which is generally like having an outstretched arm to feel your way. I initially struggled with this as it was difficult putting all my trust in a dog. Would she really keep me safe? It takes a while to build up the necessary trust when you first put your safety in the hands (or should that be 'paws') of a dog. You suddenly wonder if it is possible for a dog to be trained to look after a person. And I often wondered in the early days if I was a suitable person to be a guide dog owner as generally I do like to be in control of what I do.

Another thing that I found difficult during training was that I was suddenly responsible for a dog and had to make sure that I did not put both of us in danger, for example when crossing the road. I did once have an issue in Hull when I mistakenly tried to cross a dual carriageway with Hattie and got halfway and realised my mistake. Somebody reported me to Guide Dogs and I had a chat with my Guide Dog trainer to understand where I had gone wrong. So even with a dog, it is still a good idea to accept help when offered by other people when appropriate.

Then we had a problem during training. Hattie became ill one morning and was very sick. I wondered what was wrong. Was it something that I had done? In a panic I rang Guide Dogs to tell them that Hattie was sick. The guide dog trainer said, "Let's see how she is when I visit this afternoon."

Fortunately, the sickness stopped and whilst waiting for the visit that afternoon I discovered the likely cause. During the night and without my knowledge, Hattie had helped herself to a 3kg bag of cat food.

This turned out to be the first of many stealing incidents involving Hattie.

The better news was that upon completion of the training we qualified and I became a Guide Dog owner working with a sweet but crazy dog called Hattie.

Guide dogs do not charge owners for a dog but you do pay 50p when you sign the contract. I could never have afforded a guide dog as it costs in the region of £50,000 to train a dog. It is thanks to you, the public, that these dogs make dreams come true and give independence to people like me.

Over the next few weeks, it was like taking your baby out for the first time. People were so pleased when they greeted us. I was the proud owner of beautiful Hattie.

A bond developed between Hattie and me and she reacted to my moods. It takes a few months to create such a bond, and for a few weeks Hattie spent as much time with me as possible, and had a basket in my bedroom where she slept. I was pleased when she eventually chose to sleep downstairs, particularly as Hattie could snore for England. I was once having a relaxing facial in a beauty salon where they had soft music on in the background. Hattie was so relaxed that she fell asleep and her snoring was loud enough to drown out the music.

When I was nervous, it affected her work; when I was happy and joyful she became a bit crazy. This bond grew over the first few months. I knew deep down we both adored each other.

Hattie soon started to give me confidence. The hardest thing to learn was not to adore Hattie so much that she became the boss. The guide dog owner must be the one giving instructions to the dog.

The great thing was that if I ordered Hattic to go forward and cross a road and she recognised a danger such as a car approaching that I hadn't heard, she was trained to disobey the order. How amazing is that? To this day I still can't get over what these dogs can do.

As you are probably aware, you can take a guide dog anywhere, and it is against the law to refuse access. It is my own personal choice, but I never take Hattie into the dentist's clinical area and instead leave her with the receptionist. Otherwise the clinical area has to be cleaned before the next patient can be treated. I also avoided taking Hattie into toilet cubicles, but this was because she had an annoying habit of drinking water from the toilet bowl.

As I stated earlier, Hattie was a master thief. Many things were stolen, from ten pound notes and tea towels to a whole birthday cake in the shape of a guide dog that had been made especially for me. She even stole a sandwich out of a lady's bag whilst at an Open University study day.

Her passion was the Woolworths' pick and mix counter. It took me a few visits to fully understand why she took me via the back of the shop when we were leaving. I soon realised it was her passion for cherry lips sweets and dolly mixtures!

The first Christmas that I had Hattie I was given some Thorntons' chocolates as a gift. The brightly wrapped sweets soon went missing. And as you have probably already guessed, we soon had sparkly wrappers being passed in the garden.

To keep the thief in check, we soon changed our habits and put a child-proof gate across the kitchen door and made sure there were no bins around for Hattie to steal from.

One thing I have always said about Hattie is that she worked hard but also played hard. She could win Oscars for some of her dramatic performances. Yet she won the hearts of so many people in my home town of Beverley.

There was never a dull moment and lots of people grew to love us. If I was having a day when I was feeling a little down, we would take a walk into the town where we always received a warm welcome.

I loved chatting to people about my amazing dog. I was once in the town chatting to an elderly lady and she got upset. I found out that her dog had not long since died. I took her for a coffee in a café and we had a lovely chat. I then had to ring my daughter on the way home and explained that I was running late as I had been kidnapped by a lady.

Over time, my children have got used to me helping others. This was the nursing side of me coming out. It was great to be caring me again. I thrive on caring and it was like the light at the end of a dark tunnel. I could still be me.

I have many stories that I could tell you about Hattie but all together they would be a book in themselves. But I will share a few more with you.

One day I was walking down the street listening to my talking sat nav which was giving me directions on where to go. Suddenly, I got a tap on the shoulder that made me jump. The lady who was trying to get my attention then said, "Can I just say it's amazing what guide dogs can do. I heard her telling you where to go." To ensure Guide Dogs were then not going to get lots of requests for talking dogs like the one in Beverley, I did explain to this lady that it was me using a sat nav.

Also, I have been asked many times, 'is that a blind dog'? and I often think, 'I hope not, she could see this morning', whilst politely replying, "It's me who is blind, not the dog."

Once in a train station I overheard a lady saying to a friend, "That poor dog, it's blind."

People often talk to the guide dog and not the person. I have actually had people give the dog instructions to pass to me.

Someone once asked, "Does your dog answer your phone?" Please don't ring me to try this one.

I soon started to wonder, 'How can I show my appreciation for being given this amazing dog? How can I help others receive this gift'? Well there wasn't a fundraising group in Beverley so I helped the team in Hull, which is some 13 miles away. When the opportunity came to start a Beverley group, I jumped at the chance and became the chairman of the Beverley Guide Dogs branch. This involved arranging fundraising collections and helping volunteers learn more about guide dogs. Best of all I became a speaker for Guide Dogs. I loved to tell groups about the adventures that I had with Hattie.

One example was how Hattie enabled me to be a normal mum taking my young child, Jamie, to his first day at primary school. I was so proud to be taking him. I would not have liked to have to send him with a helper. I have been into schools and visited Scout and Girl Guide groups talking about my guide dog. And the children ask such lovely questions. And the odd funny ones. One little boy asked if I couldn't see well and then he explained very carefully how glasses worked.

'Does Hattie carry your shopping'? And 'can Hattie go inside of McDonalds'? The answer is 'yes' but we had to be careful as often people leave chips on the floor and Hattie would enjoy eating them.

I will never get tired of sharing my guide dog stories.

Quite often when I would walk into a room or a pub, somebody would say, "Isn't she beautiful!" I always replied, "Thank you very much," knowing they meant Hattie ... but it is nice being called beautiful.

I was nominated by Beverley Guide Dogs' group for an award for 'Inspirational Guide Dog Owner of the Year', one of a series of annual awards organised by Guide Dogs. I never expected to be selected as one of the three finalists but I was and we were invited to the awards ceremony in London. Prior to the event, the Daily Express ran a feature on me and the two other nominees and our pictures and life stories appeared in the paper.

Both Hattie and I had makeovers so we looked our best and I bought a new evening dress for the occasion as it was a 'black tie' event held in central London. It was a great chance to talk to other guide dog owners and hear their amazing stories. Whilst we did not win the award, I was still very proud to be the first person from the Yorkshire & Humber area to be invited to attend the evening and be up for an award. I have a number of professional photos taken during the evening which remind me of the great partnership that Hattie and I had formed.

STARTING THE VisAbility CHARITY

Meeting other VI people at Goalball had made me realise that there were other local people with visual issues who were determined to get the most out of life. I quickly saw the benefits of getting involved in activities that brought VI people like myself together and allowed us opportunities to enjoy ourselves. This provided the inspiration and motivation that led to me forming a visibility charity with the specific aim of providing sports and leisure activities for visually impaired people.

I also was curious to see how other VIs managed day-to-day tasks, particularly those who were mothers as well. I had many questions such as how do you push a pram? How do you track a moving toddler in the house? ... and many more...

There was (and still is) a local blind charity that offered a day centre service where food and other basics were provided but it was aimed at an older age group. I felt there was a need for something else that a day centre was unable to offer.

On a personal level, I wanted to avoid the feeling of being isolated and the only one struggling with being a VI mum.

Being a VI mum in a school playground is very difficult. As you are unable to do eye contact it is very, very hard to make friends. It helped knowing that other VI mums went through the same issues.

As soon I discussed my idea for a way forward with other VIs, their responses gave me the confidence to go through with it and I decided I was prepared to go to the lengths of forming a charity. I must admit I didn't realise how difficult or how time-consuming it was going to be. A few tears were shed along the way.

Forming a properly funded charity would also enable us to arrange funding for interesting and unusual activities such as paragliding which excited me. I found alternative ideas such as arranging a coffee morning for VI friends a bit too mundane.

And in the background was the desire I have mentioned previously that I didn't want people caring for me.

I also didn't want just to sit at home and do nothing. I'm not a great fan of daytime TV. I must admit I have always needed to get outside as sitting inside all day would soon get me down. I didn't want to go back into the sort of deep depression that I experienced in my younger years so it was very important to me to move on. I do know that many newly VI people do get very down and struggle to leave the house and I can really understand why.

The first step was to form a Board of Trustees who would oversee the charity. We completed the statutory paperwork and the VisAbility charity was born – charity number 1127286.

We then applied to National Lottery and other funding outlets for grants in order to start activities. Applying for grants was not always easy as most require a lot of form filling; not easy when you are VI.

One fundraising idea we tried was supermarket bag packing although we did find that some people, rather than have bags packed by someone with a guide dog or white cane, perhaps understandably preferred to pack their own bags. But they were still kind enough to put money in our collection box and so it raised useful funds for the charity. It was always great to talk about the charity and people were amazed when I told them that we did rifle shooting, indoor rock climbing and more!

The charity has really taken off and grown over the years. Its existence caused a real buzz amongst local VIs. I was genuinely surprised at how many VI people lived locally. At least I wasn't the only one! You just don't know how many people with the same issues are in your own town or nearby towns.

To help identify activities that people wanted to undertake, we sent out a questionnaire to local VI people asking for feedback on the types of activities they would like. It was no good booking rock climbing if people didn't want to do it. I soon found out trying to do questionnaires for blind people was difficult, as most can't read print. A lot of the older members couldn't use email. The best way was often to ring round to find the answers although this was often time-consuming especially as we all liked to talk.

To help advertise the charity we put up posters at the eye clinics in local hospitals. However, not all VI people need to go to the eye clinic.

The local radio was amazing and I got to speak on the radio about the charity. Also we made the local newspapers. These were exciting times for the charity.

One early activity we arranged was to take people out for a supervised paragliding session. The night before I lay awake for much of the night and I was so nervous about doing it. When I arrived, one of the younger VIs came up to me and said that he had also been awake for much of the night, although in his case it was because he was so excited at having the opportunity to try paragliding. It was so inspiring to see other VIs having a great time and getting excellent feedback on the activities.

Doing activities that would normally be thought as not suitable for a VI person also helped us all build our confidence.

Filling out the required Health and Safety risk assessments was very difficult. Everything we did had to be safe. In particular, safeguards during VI archery had to be strict to ensure safety for all.

Over the years, we have had some amazing coaches who were both understanding and ensured our safety at the same time.

I even got to fly a small plane. This was arranged with the pilot training school at our local airfield at Leven. Before having my go, I sent a text to my mum and said, 'this is your pilot speaking'. I'm not sure who was the most nervous - me or my mum. With help from the airfield, we made dreams come true for VI people who enjoyed flying. This also led to me being featured on the BBC's 'Songs of Praise' when it came to Beverley. This was a moment that made my parents very proud and it was also great fun filming for television.

In terms of the activities we have organised, they have included 10-pin bowling, archery, art, blind cricket, brewery trips, choir, cookery, cycling in the park, drama, football golf, golf, parents' groups, rifle shooting, rock climbing, sailing, sea fishing, walking groups and general day trips out.

Many of the teachers that I was able to bring in to lead the groups were VI themselves. I quickly realised that not only was it good for the group but also great for the well-being of the person teaching.

I also arranged first aid training for the group. I saw this as being very important, especially for a VI parent who may have an issue with a sick child. For example, they need to know what to do if the child suddenly starts choking. There is a need for first aid training for VI people as it is not covered at blind school and courses run by the local St John's Ambulance group were not accessible for everyone. Many of the group worked up to the 'first aid at work' certificate and I was very proud of them. A couple of members went on to do voluntary work with St John's. How amazing is that?

We also had a reflexology training group where VI people were taught to try reflexology. This involved the VI going away and practising their new found skills on their friends and families. We all found it amazing and again good for our well-being as we were able to help others.

People who are involved in charity come from a wide-range of backgrounds, lifestyles and ages. There are people who have been VI from birth. Some of them attended blind schools but others went through mainstream education. Then there are people who have lost their sight at some point but have retained a passion for life. I would like to think that I was able to help encourage that passion. Part of our mission statement states that we want to help VI people and their families climb their highest mountain.

Our youngest active member was pre-school age whilst the oldest invited us to his birthday party when he was 100 years old. Sadly, he passed away shortly after reaching that milestone.

We were also lucky to have the support of some fantastic volunteers. I was able to raise the charity's profile through radio interviews and other media coverage. I guess people could see our passion. My own family were very supportive and my daughter and her husband have been involved as volunteers.

This is not the place to thank people individually as there are so many people who have contributed to the charity's success. I won't name individuals, and indeed there are too many to name, but they know who they are.

After five years, we started a shop. It was an amazing project. It fulfilled my vision for VI people to be able to help themselves and the shop raises funds to enable us to do this. The shop not only sells clothes and bric-a-brac, but also paintings by local VI artists who are involved with the charity. We also sell re-claimed furniture that people have donated and which our VIs have fixed and repaired. It was a good idea to have a shop on the high street. People began to realise we were a local charity helping local people.

The charity also had its own award-winning garden which was created and then looked after by the VIs. It was started after I arranged for a demonstration from a lady on how to pot plants. People were keen to put what they had learned into practice. So we identified a small space of land behind the charity's building in Hull at the time, which was just rubble and soil and where nothing had grown for years.

The ideas for the garden came in from lots of people. One was for a glass stone wall where people each created a glass stone during a craft activity. The glass bricks were then put together form a wall. We used safety glass, of course. The garden received a lot of praise and we were delighted in particular to win a 'Blooming Hull' award.

A lot of the VI people did not own a garden so it was nice to have a garden growing our own vegetables and some nice smelling plants. It is a great area for picnics and barbeques to be enjoyed with friends and family.

The VisAbility charity is my great passion and something I will never forget. It has helped heal many wounds for me and many others. I have made and met many friends. When I look back it was something that came out of a disastrous time of my life when I lost my sight. However, I have had the time of my life and have met some wonderful people.

The charity shop is still open and located in Hessle Road, Hull and money raised goes to provide equipment for VI people. We no longer undertake activities as this need is now fulfilled by another local blind charity.

I will end by saying how grateful I am to everyone who shared my vision for the charity and helped me make it happen.

FIRST DEALINGS WITH THE RNIB

The first time I dealt with the RNIB (Royal National Institute for the Blind) and realised how their work really helps VI people was many years before I lost my sight. Shortly after I had started working, I used one of my first pay-packets to buy my sister Michelle a video of The Wizard of Oz with audio description from the RNIB. This helped Michelle, who you may recall was blind from birth, enjoy one of her favourite films. At the time audio description wasn't available like it is on TV today.

When you lose your sight, the RNIB are obviously one of the first charities you think of. In the early days, I found their online shop really useful and started buying different aids to make life easier. I also received some information leaflets telling me about sight loss.

One of the first things that I bought from the RNIB was a colour detector. This scans items and tells you its colour and is very useful for a single mum when you are sorting dirty washing and don't want to mix whites and dark colours! It was also very useful in helping Jamie learn about colours.

What I really longed for was to read a biography about somebody's life after sight loss but I couldn't find any and this was the seed that started me thinking, 'one day I will write a book'.

The RNIB also provided audio books for my Open University course. Initially I struggled being unable to read books as I love reading and having access to audio books gave me back my love of books.

I was given a 'DAISY player'. This is a complete audio substitute for printed material designed for use by VI people and others who have difficulty reading traditional printed output. I used it to read the audio books that I got through RNIB. These were a mix of everyday books as well as study books. It took a while to get used to audio books and I often found that I fell asleep and it carried on talking. I soon learnt to put a timer on so it stopped, which solved this problem.

Little did I realise at this stage that I would get more involved with the RNIB in due course.

Independently of the RNIB and to help with my Open University course, I did a braille correspondence course as originally the course work that I received was in braille format. As a result, I can read basic stage 1 braille. By 'basic' I mean that I would struggle to read a letter in braille. Also I am very slow. So reading a braille book would be beyond my level.

My interest with the RNIB grew further when the local area RNIB campaigns' coordinator came along to speak to members of my Visibility charity about campaigning for VI rights. I became very passionate about this. As soon as she started telling us about campaign work I could see that this was something I would love to be involved in. I wanted a voice and joining the RNIB campaigns group would give me opportunities to help and voice my opinions.

Through campaigns run by the RNIB I have subsequently met many inspirational people and heard so many stories about how other people were campaigning around the UK. I then realised that I wasn't the only person out there who was passionate about VI issues. This has been an important part of my life and in its own way has helped me rebuild my life.

Meeting some of the people involved in RNIB campaigns was a real bonus and a life-changing moment for me. I soon learnt a lot about campaigning – how to lobby MPs and local councils and how to run a small campaigns' group.

In my experience, the RNIB do an amazing job by running so many different campaigns. The RNIB work in so many areas and campaign on behalf of all VI people, whether blind from birth or people who lose sight later in life.

Their support helpline for VI people is also very valuable. Looking back to when I bought that video with audio description for Michelle, life has certainly improved since then for VI people because when I now go to the cinema I can get an audio description via headphones for any film that I want to see. The RNIB have been involved in many of these changes.

There have been numerous other successful RNIB campaigns that have made life easier for VIs. For example, they worked with Barclays Bank on the development of 'talking' cash machines with an audio description function that can be heard when you plug headphones into a socket on the cash machine.

In terms of technology, RNIB are very good at moving with the times. Their helpline now offers technical advice on how a VI person can get the most out of modern gadgets such as iPhones.

The RNIB also supported the change from Disability Living Allowance to Personal Independence Payments (PIP). The RNIB was involved in the development of PIP and I was invited to stand on a stage and take part in a presentation to MPs, civil servants and the media on the subject.

At the same presentation, I also explained that every day can be different for a VI person. The example that I used was walking a route along a normal everyday street that you use on a regular basis. One day you can walk down the street and there are no obstacles on the pavement. But the next day it could have cars parked on it or wheelie bins blocking your path. No pavement is the same one day to the next.

I also remember telling them why VI people need help. There were chuckles from the audience when I told them that I once went into my bathroom and picked up a tube of what I thought was toothpaste to find I was using hair removal cream. This was the reaction I was hoping for as people always remember humour.

The RNIB also support people claiming benefits. People often lose their jobs at the same time as sight loss occurs and it is really essential to know what and when you can claim. So quite a big part of the advice service from RNIB is the help and support they offer you on how to make your claim for benefits.

This also includes assistance with filling in forms. I used family and friends but it would have been easier to use an RNIB adviser who could have assisted with completing the forms, which can be done either by telephone or with a personal visit depending on the situation. If there is no RNIB person available in the area, they will contact a local blind charity and arrange for them to visit you.

I wish I had used the RNIB's services more at the start of my sight loss. In particular, I hadn't realised that they provide emotional as well as practical support. Being able to talk with someone who had been through sight loss would have calmed my early fears about being VI for the rest of my life.

I also hadn't realised that the RNIB also supports friends and family and I think this would have been very useful for Ella in particular and also possibly for my mum. What you don't realise in the first few weeks and months after sight loss is how much it affects those around you. The RNIB advice line is open for anyone to use, no matter what their relationship is to the VI person. For example, a teacher can use the service if one of their pupils is VI.

Being involved with RNIB campaigns has certainly increased my confidence and has given me the passion to ensure that my future working life involves making life better for others in similar situations.

INTERNET DATING AS A VI

In my experience, in general it is more difficult for VIs to meet the opposite sex as making eye contact is not easy. So when you are in a busy pub it is much more difficult to see if you have caught someone's eye.

At times I have wished that people were seeing me, Dianne, before they saw that poor blind lady. I have had people talk to me in a very loud, slow voice. It sometimes seems that on meeting me for the first time, date or no date, that some people are not sure where to start a conversation. It's like my sight can cause a physical barrier.

Here's an example of what I mean and how easily mistakes can happen. I was once in a pub that my friend owns. It was the end of April and the first sunny Sunday after the winter. The bar was busy and my friend was busy serving as fast as she could. Hattie was asleep tucked away near my feet. Then a man came in from the beer garden and pushed to the front of the bar not far from me. He wanted serving fast and was getting grumpy over having to wait. I knew my friend was doing her best so I quietly explained to Mr Impatient that he had to wait in the queue. I then made a comment, "Are you in such a rush to get back in the garden to improve your sun tan?"

This was where the real problem started. He got very upset and angry with this statement. I had said it in jest and couldn't understand what had caused such offence and why he was getting so angry. Fortunately, my friend saw the problem and came to the rescue. "Dianne, you have just told a black man that he needs to suntan." And then she turned to the man and said, "This is my friend Dianne. She is blind. That is her guide dog, Hattie, near her feet."

He then started apologising and we both ended up laughing at ourselves. So this is my own personal example of how meeting people for the first time can cause confusion.

I had heard about internet dating on daytime TV and thought that it would be worth giving it a try so I registered with a free dating website (www.plentyoffish). I took a few weeks to think about whether I should sign up. Was it right for me? How safe was it? I didn't want to meet up with a married man who was looking for one night stands, or any man just looking for sex. I wanted to find someone to have a loving relationship with.

It must have taken me at least ten attempts to write my profile. I have included the finished article at the end of the chapter. It was also a difficult choice to decide on a recent photograph of myself to use. I made a conscious decision not to mention being VI in the profile itself. This was partly not to make myself too vulnerable and also because I wanted people to have the chance to get to know Dianne the person before they knew I was VI. I didn't want my sight to be the first thing they found out about me.

Once my profile went on the dating website, people started contacting me and we used email to find out if we were likely to be a suitable match. Learning to read between the lines became very useful.

On at least two occasions, once I had disclosed that I was registered blind, the other party didn't want to get involved further. I was obviously disappointed at being rejected, especially if it was because I was VI and not because of any personality trait. This put me off for a while as they were quite happy to talk and looking forward to meeting up until they found out I was VI. This affected my confidence and made me feel I was less of a person. I can understand why some people react this way, especially when there are plenty of fish in the sea.

I felt it was only fair to let people know about my sight before we met. Otherwise it would definitely be a 'blind date' when your date turns up and you only find out then that they are blind.

I wasn't against the idea of dating another VI although I didn't expect it would be easy to find a VI on a dating website. In fact, the reason why I have never dated a VI man is simply lack of opportunity.

I will never forget my first internet date as it was when Hattie was a bit naughty.

My date had stated that he was in his early 40s. His profile and emails were very romantic and I started to think that 'he could be the one'. I told him that I couldn't see very well and indeed he generally seemed very pleased about that and I soon realised why.

When we met for a meal for two, it turned out he was an awful lot older than his profile picture. It took me a while to work that out with my limited vision. Furthermore, his false teeth didn't fit very well and you could hear them chattering throughout the meal.

After the meal, we moved to sit in more comfortable chairs and enjoy a bottle of wine. As he leant forward to pour us both a glass of wine, his toupee fell off onto the floor. Hattie obviously thought it was a rabbit and so tried to kill it. When I eventually got the gentleman's hair piece off Hattie, it was covered in dog slaver and I had to hand it back to him in this state. I am not sure who was the most embarrassed. At this point and to avoid any doubt, I just thanked him and advised him we wouldn't be meeting up again.

On another date I met a guy initially just for coffee at a café. He wanted me to stay on and have some food with him but one of the staff who knew me had a word in my ear and made me aware that he was well-known locally for having one night stands. So he was sent on his way.

Being on a dating site is like being on an emotional roller-coaster. I soon learned not to worry about rejection and indeed that sometimes I needed to be tough and be the one saying "no". Being VI made me look more at the person within rather than any initial impression from their photograph on the site.

I was always conscious of ensuring my own safety. Indeed, anyone going out internet dating needs to consider these issues. My system was to get a friend to ring me at a pre-agreed point to check that everything was fine. She once helped me out of a bad date by phoning mid-way through and I pretended she was giving me bad news and I needed to get home straightaway. I never gave out my home address and would only meet in a public place. I also took a while before arranging the initial meeting.

In general as VI, you do feel a bit more vulnerable and present a bit more of a challenge to other people.

Though I must say, having given internet dating a go, I have enjoyed the experience, and I am still friends with some of the people that I met via the dating website.

So should VI people go on dating sites? What would I advise after my experience? I am no expert but VI people need love the same as any other person using the site. I found it better not to state publicly on my profile that I'm VI. It's certainly not that I am embarrassed about it but I felt it kept me safe from people taking advantage of my lack of sight.

And if you are VI and have experienced rejections on dating websites because of your sight, I know how you must be feeling about it. But don't give up! Some people are unsure about how to even talk to a VI person. Keep looking and I'm sure you will find a soul-mate who accepts you for who you are. I eventually did, but that's a story for another time.

And finally a word of caution for all you ladies, based on experience. If a man is very keen to send you a photograph, then get your best friend rather than your teenage daughter to look at it first. It may not be a photograph of his lovely face. Some men think sending photographs of their manhood is acceptable behaviour. Gentleman, it is not. Please stop doing it.

My dating website profile

Do you drink? - Socially
Marital Status - Single
Profession - Management
Smarts - Graduate degree
Do you want children? - Does not want children
Do you do drugs? - No
Do you have children? – Yes
Do you have a car? - N/A
About me: Well I like to laugh. I have a strange sense of humour. Music - I love all kinds - Eric Clapton, blues, most music but not really into heavy rock. I really enjoy my life and just looking for that someone special to share happy and sad times with. I am a real romantic. I am unique. My friends will tell you there is only one of me. So this is a once in a lifetime offer, don't let this pass you by. Sorry told you I had a strange sense of humour!!
Ideal date: have a good conversation while holding hands drinking a nice glass of wine. Maybe a kiss at the end of the date. PS Please note I DO NOT DO ONE NIGHT STANDS OR TWO!

IT'S ALWAYS COLOURFUL
IN OUR HOUSE
(written by my daughter, Ella)

I decided to use the title of 'It's always colourful in our house' for my chapter as it is a phrase that my mum often uses herself.

For me, this one sentence sums up life with Mum. It shows that our family life could be eventful and difficult at times. Secondly, and more importantly, it shows that she is always positive and does not let the hard times get her down.

When planning this chapter, it was difficult to decide where to begin as there are so many things that I could say about Mum. However, I would like it to be about the most important lesson that I have learnt from her. This is, although at times life can seem to be one big struggle, it's best to tackle problems head on, stay positive and make the most of a bad situation.

I hope that this chapter will show that Mum never gives up and pushes herself to keep on going even when things get tough. She has a knack of making some good come from the bad stuff and she was just the same when she lost her sight.

The starting point for my story is when Mum got ill with meningitis because although a lot happened before this event, this is when I remember our life as a family really changing.

I can recall Mum saying she had a headache and was going for a nap. A while later when I went to check on her, I found that she would not wake up. I rolled her towards me in an attempt to bring her from her sleep as at this point I had assumed she was just in a deep sleep. When I rolled her over, I found that she was hot and clammy. She started to speak but the words she was saying did not make sense. Immediately I knew there was something wrong.

As I was young, I panicked and did not know what to do. So I ran to a neighbour's house to ask for help and together we decided to ring '999'. At first the person on the phone seemed quite calm but after we explained that Mum was a diabetic they sent an ambulance to check her over. When the medics arrived I could tell that the situation was serious by the way they were speaking and it became a blur as Mum was rushed away to hospital. I was left worrying and wondering if she would come back and if things would ever be the same again.

Mum had to spend some time recovering in hospital as she had meningitis and was obviously very ill although she wanted to come home straightaway to be with us.

When she came home she insisted that we should carry on as we normally would and put the incident behind us. Mum was determined not to let the situation affect us because that is the kind of woman she is. The kind of woman who just carries on no matter what happens and does all she can to make sure her children are not affected by her difficulties.

It seemed that our family life would not have to change at all. But of course as you will have already read, things did have to change...

The next big event happened a while later. Things had settled down, we had just been on a lovely family holiday and everything seemed quite 'normal' (if there is such a thing as 'normal'. I'm not convinced there is). I clearly remember having an average morning, sitting in my room, straightening my hair ready to go out and Mum walking in to announce, "Ella I don't want to worry you but I can't see anything!!"

She seemed quite cheery and we both decided that her sight would return. How wrong we were! I happily helped Mum to get the boys up and ready and we did our best to get on with our day. However, as the day passed her sight did not improve. Mum began to realise that she needed to seek help and face the thought that she may never see again.

In the early days, it was very difficult for me and my brothers and Mum to adapt to her sight loss. We found that the simple things which she had taken for granted such as making a cup of tea, walking to the local shop and using a telephone were all becoming difficult for her. My brother Jo and I had to step up and make these things possible again. We also had to make sure that the house was safe for Mum. This meant making sure that everything was always away in its place such as shoes and toys and looking out for dangers such as water being spilt on the floor.

When going out, we had to get use to guiding Mum. It was tricky at first as we would often accidentally walk her into doorways, run off to look at things and leave her stranded in the middle of a shop or forget to tell her when we were going up a step or crossing a busy road.

However, I think we found it more difficult not being able to rely on Mum being able to drive us around. When we went to see our friends or to school Mum would have usually taken us. As we still had friends in Hull, we had to get used to using public transport to take us to see them. This was quite scary at first, as we had not had to use it before. Worst of all, we knew Mum was not happy. She wanted to be independent. She did not want me and my brothers to have to look after her and she did not want to rely on others just to do a food shop or take my youngest brother into town for a treat.

She was lost in a world with no sight and she struggled to adapt to a life where she was not able to carry out the simplest of tasks on her own. This was not my mum. She was a strong woman who thought through everything and never gave up. I began to worry that through losing her sight she had lost herself as well. But she did fight to get her freedom back.

Things improved slightly when she was given her cane. Once she had been taught to use it, she was able to snatch back a small amount of her freedom. Mum gathered a lot of courage and started to make small trips out on her own.

I will always remember the day she tried to go to the local shops on her own. Not long after she had left, I had a phone call from her. Mum was panicking as she had taken a wrong turn and become disorientated. She was now frightened, lost and alone in a crowded place not daring to move through fear of being knocked over or walking into something. I rushed out full of worry to find her and bring her home safely. After that event I often worried about her when she insisted on going out on her own.

Mum was searching for ways she could claim some independence and she found a big chunk of it in her first guide dog, 'Hattie'. It was a long wait to get a guide dog but eventually she was paired with Hattie and was trained to use her. As soon as Mum was given Hattie, we could see that she was happy and ready to do things independently.

Once they had passed their training, Mum chose to go out on a small trip to our local shops with Hattie to get a coffee. We all stayed at home nervous and eagerly awaiting her return. A lot of time passed and I began to worry that she had got lost. In the end I decided to ring her and find out what was taking her so long. I didn't want Mum to think I was checking up on her, but I had to know she was all right. I was shocked and amazed to find that she had got on a train and travelled to our local beach to get an ice cream. Apparently, when walking past the train station she had decided that she wanted to prove to herself that she could make an even more adventurous trip. But that is my mum, give her a small slice of freedom and she will multiply it.

As she worked with Hattie, her confidence just kept growing. It was amazing to see her relaxing and able to do things herself again. It was also wonderful to not need to worry about Mum going out alone anymore. We knew she was in safe hands (well, paws) when she left the house.

Mum started to look for places where she could meet other visually impaired people. She had found an online forum where she was able to speak to other visually impaired mums. This site was so useful as it had offered her support as a VI mum. She was able to share her problems and fears with people in similar situations. She was also able to learn new coping techniques from the other mums. For example, she had learnt that she could get a pram that she could pull behind her so that she could take my little brother out for a walk. She also learnt that some visually impaired mums put a bell on their toddler so they can hear where they are. She now wanted to meet other visually impaired people locally so they could support each other.

Unfortunately, at this time the only local group for visually impaired people was aimed at people a lot older than Mum and they did not run any activities that she was interested in. As a result, Mum decided to help launch a new local group aimed at visually impaired people of all ages and abilities. This group offered a range of activities including; Goalball (a form of football for the blind) archery, rifle shooting, race car driving, arts and craft, rock climbing, gliding, sailing, cricket and more.

Mum has put many years into planning and running activities for this group. As a result, many visually impaired people have had a safe place to support one another and learn that losing your sight is not the end of your journey it is just the beginning of a new one and that, even with a visual impairment there are still many things you can achieve. This group is just one of the things that shows me that she can make hardships into success.

Through losing her sight, Mum has been able to help many others. She is also helping other visually impaired people by working with the Royal National Institute for the Blind. She runs campaigns locally and is able to help people nationally as well. Mum does all she can to remove barriers for visually impaired people and make life more manageable for them.

Overall, although life has sometimes been tough, I will always remember how hard Mum has fought to regain her independence and to keep her family happy. She has made the best of a bad situation for sure. She has made her sight loss work for the better and has helped many people as a result. Therefore, one important lesson I have learnt from her is don't let life get you down. 'When life gives you lemons, make lemonade' as they say!

I hope that I can follow this lesson for the rest of my life. And I hope that, through learning about my mum's journey, she can help you as well.

THAT'S <u>NOT</u> ALL FOLKS

The previous chapters have covered my story up to 2010.

I have continued to receive plenty of media exposure, one of the highlights being getting a call out of the blue which led to me appearing on BBC's 'Songs of Praise'. Little did I know that it would take so long to film six minutes' worth of TV.

I also appeared on the ITV local news programme as part of an 'A-Boards' campaign that I set up in the Yorkshire and Humber area, which was then taken up by the RNIB to highlight problems caused by advertising boards on pavements.

A low point came when I had a scary experience on a train with Hattie and for a while lost my sense of independence. The good news is that I eventually got it back.

There have been changes on the guide dog front as well. We noticed that Hattie was getting tired and was no longer capable of being a working guide dog and the decision was made by Guide Dogs to stop her working in 2014. She now lives in happy retirement with my daughter Ella and her husband. It felt like a first child leaving home and I found losing her very difficult.

After a 12-month gap, I got a new guide dog, Darcy, who is a bundle of energy and has taken over where Hattie left off. Darcy is pictured with me on the cover of the book.

Another highlight of my life since 2010 was being there as my first grandchild, Benjamin came into the world in 2015. I regret that I am not able to push him around in a pram but I chose not to get a pram that I am able to pull. I am just grateful that I survived the meningitis and am around to watch him grow up.

I had some success with my online dating search and I'll go into more detail on this in my next book!

I have also rekindled a long lost love ... for cricket. I have played Blind Cricket and have been interviewed by Jonathan Agnew for a programme about VI people and sport on Radio Five Live. The latter covered what I loved about being part of a cricket crowd, enjoying the atmosphere and following the action by listening to the BBC radio commentary. And no trip to a cricket ground is complete without an ice cream, which you will find out from following my Facebook page, is my favourite treat!

I have also become a modern day diabetic, trying out the latest medical technology to help manage my condition on a daily basis. As a result of research, the treatment and management of diabetes has come a long way since I was diagnosed with it at the age of 13 in 1981.

I have so many things I'd like to share with you, about my diabetes, my sight loss, my charity and my goals for the future. As I learnt from my parents as a young girl, life never brings you more than you can handle. Yes, it's been tough but I was determined to find a way to make my life, and my children's lives, as normal as possible. There is always a way.

I look forward to sharing with you more about my journey in my second book which will be available early in 2017.

FURTHER INFORMATION

Throughout the book, I have mentioned several organisations that supported me throughout my life. If any of these issues have affected you, or a loved one, I urge you to contact them. The support they provide is a vital service and can help you and your loved one at a time of uncertainty and vulnerability.

****

Meningitis UK

The website for Meningitis UK is www.meningitis.org where meningitis symptoms are listed. They also have a free telephone helpline - 0800 8800 3344

Guide Dogs

To find out the about your local Guide Dogs branch, please visit www.guidedogs.org.uk, telephone 0118 983 5555 or email guidedogs@guidedogs.org.uk.

To sponsor a guide dog puppy (and enable a blind or partially sighted person to enjoy the same freedom of movement as everyone else) please use the website above or telephone 0800 953 0113.

Royal National Institute for Blind People

For more information on the excellent information and support that RNIB can provide to VI people, please visit their website www.rnib.org.uk

To contact RNIB's emotional support service, please call 0303 123 9999 or email helpline@rnib.org.uk

Dianne Woodford, Author

To find out more about my current adventures, or to stay in touch with the progress of my next book, please get in touch through any of the following methods.

I would also be most grateful if you would leave a review of my book on Amazon.co.uk or Goodreads.com. It really helps readers to find new authors and I'm particularly keen to get my book out there to people who have suffered from mental health issues, Type 1 diabetes, adult meningitis and sight loss. If my story can help just one person, I will feel blessed.

Lots of Love,

Dianne

www.diannewoodford.co.uk

www.facebook.com/diannewoodfordtheauthor

www.twitter.com/@authorDianneW

ACKNOWLEDGEMENTS

I would like to acknowledge the support and assistance from the following people who helped make my vision for writing this book a reality:

My partner and co-author, Jim McIntosh who made sense of my words and showed great patience and understanding to ensure the book reflects all aspects of my life story.

My editor, Sue Miller (www.allwordsmatter.co.uk) for her ongoing support and encouragement and taking me through the process of publishing a book step by step.

Cover designer, Alan Jones for creating a striking image which is partly out of focus, and obscured by black dots. This is how I have seen the world since 2007.

Photographer, Gina Rayment, (ginarphotography.strikingly.com) who took some great pictures of myself and Darcy on Beverley Westwood, one of which is used on the book cover.

Phil Burrows for design and maintenance of my website (www.diannewoodford.co.uk) and going the extra mile to make it easily accessible for VI people.

Ella, Jo and Jamie, my son-in-law Dean and all my family and friends.

Frank McFarlane for his friendship and support through my sight loss journey.

The RNIB and Guide Dogs for the Blind.

DIANNE - A BRIEF BIOGRAPHY

Born in 1968, Dianne was brought up in her parents' house in Hull with her three older sisters, a younger brother and her adopted blind sister. She was diagnosed with type 1 diabetes as a teenager.

Dianne left school at the age of 16 and enjoyed a 23-year career in caring and nursing, working in homes and hospitals in and around Hull and East Yorkshire.

2007 was Dianne's own 'annus horribilis' as she caught meningitis and this, together with complications stemming from her diabetes, led to her losing most of her sight in the August of that year. She is now registered blind.

A single mother of three children, she set up her own charity 'VisAbility' to help other visually impaired (VI) people in Hull and East Yorkshire and Dianne now works with RNIB on campaigns to improve the lives of VI people.

Dianne now lives in the historic town of Beverley with her children, her retired guide dog Hattie and a current guide dog Darcy, pet dog Bob and three cats. She describes her house as always being colourful.

She is the sort of visually impaired person who will let an old lady help her across a road that she actually doesn't want to cross, and will then wait for the old lady to disappear and will cross back on her own so as to not upset anybody's feelings.

www.diannewoodford.co.uk

www.facebook.com/diannewoodfordtheauthor

www.twitter.com/@authorDianneW

TESTIMONY

From David Aldwinckle, Head of Community Engagement at RNIB

"Dianne Woodford is an amazing woman. In the time that I have known her she has let nothing get in the way of her seizing the day and making the most of her life. Her sight loss is just part of who she is, and after spending time with her I am always inspired by her positive outlook, sense of humour and ability to pick herself up and go at life again. All of us, regardless of whether we are blind, partially sighted, or fully sighted can learn from her experiences."

60868867R00111

Made in the USA
Charleston, SC
11 September 2016